The Christian, The Arts, And Truth

The Christian, The Arts, And Truth

Regaining The Vision Of Greatness

FRANK E. GAEBELEIN

D. BRUCE LOCKERBIE - EDITOR

MULTNOMAH · PRESS
Portland, Oregon 97266

Unless otherwise indicated, Scripture quotations are from the Holy Bible, New International Version, © 1973, 1978 by the International Bible Society. Used by permission of Zondervan Bible Publishers.

Edited by Rodney L. Morris
Cover design and illustration by Britt Taylor Collins

THE CHRISTIAN, THE ARTS, AND TRUTH
© 1985 by Multnomah Press
Portland, Oregon 97266

Printed in the United States of America

Library of Congress Cataloging in Publication Data

Gaebelein, Frank Ely, 1899-
  The Christian, the arts, and truth.

  Includes indexes.
  1. Christianity and the arts.   2. Aesthetics.
I. Lockerbie, D. Bruce.   II. Title.
BR115.A8G34   1985   261.5'7   85-9005

85   86   87   88   89   90   –   10   9   8   7   6   5   4   3   2   1

To Marvin and Dorothie Goldberg,
my colleagues and mutual friends
with Frank E. Gaebelein

Contents

Foreword

In accepting the responsibility for putting together the contents of this book, I wish to make it clear that my work has been that of collector more than editor. Rather than presume to edit or refine the speeches, sermons, lectures, editorials, essays, and articles found among Frank E. Gaebelein's papers, I have instead allowed his words to speak for themselves. Only the most minimal, most obviously necessary alterations—such as references to the passage of time as "two years ago"—have been made in the interests of clarity.

Frank Gaebelein was my teacher and friend, as well as my administrative superior. He taught me to write and encouraged my struggle to become a writer; he criticized my work and advanced my opportunities. The least I could do in return is not tamper with his prose.

D. Bruce Lockerbie

Acknowledgments

Multnomah Press and, in particular, Rod Morris, editorial manager, encouraged me throughout the process of my putting together this collection of Frank E. Gaebelein's essays.

His daughters, Dorothy Gaebelein Hampton and Gretchen Gaebelein Hull, and son, Donn Medd Gaebelein, were especially helpful in making available to me the papers and other documents from their father's effects. They also contributed their own adult recollections of the experience of growing up as the children of Frank and Dorothy Gaebelein.

Karl E. Soderstrom, headmaster of The Stony Brook School, offered insight into the character of Frank Gaebelein, who as headmaster emeritus supported the ongoing work of his successors.

John W. Dixon, Jr., professor of religion and art at the University of North Carolina at Chapel Hill, gave generously from his store of professional expertise as well as his personal faith in providing a critical perspective on Gaebelein's work.

Harold L. Myra, publisher of *Christianity Today*, granted permission for essays originally appearing in that periodical to be republished here.

Mary Rost faithfully prepared the manuscript.

My wife Lory assisted me in numerous ways: by suggestions for the Introduction, by her loving critique of my prose, by her unfailing patience during long periods of my preoccupation with this book.

To all, my thanks.

D.B.L.

Introduction

In his later years, Frank E. Gaebelein frequently heard himself introduced—at a college in St. Paul, Minnesota, at a church in Phoenix, Arizona, at a Bible school in Portland, Oregon, at a convention of evangelical theologians in Toronto, Ontario—as "a Renaissance man." The reference intended always to convey to an audience something of Frank Gaebelein's remarkable diversity of interests and gifts. Such an introduction would cite some of these: accomplished pianist, experienced mountaineer, English stylist, astute editor, compelling preacher, self-educated Bible scholar, connoisseur of fine paintings, loving master of German shepherd dogs. The list would go on, sometimes mentioning as if only in passing what Gaebelein himself considered his singleminded passion . . . his life's work as headmaster of The Stony Brook School for forty-one years, headmaster emeritus thereafter until his death twenty years later.

A varied portfolio indeed! Yet Frank Gaebelein was no ordinary "Renaissance man." He was, instead, a modern-day Christian humanist, a designation he used for himself. According to his daughter, Gretchen Gaebelein Hull, he wrote in a 1980 letter,

> Intellectually I should describe myself as a Christian humanist. I am, of course, using the term in its classical renaissance sense, rather than in its contemporary usage, as "secular humanism," for example. I am a generalist, not a specialist, and my interests are not restricted to just one discipline.

"Christian humanist . . . secular humanism." Such terms require careful definition. In classifying himself as a Christian humanist, Gaebelein was not in any way aligning with those who deny the existence and power of a supernatural deity, those for whom time and space are the natural limits of human experience, those who regard any notion of eternity as only a fantasy. These are the premises of today's so-called "secular humanists," whose upgraded description does nothing to conceal their true identity: they are merely old-fashioned atheists with press agents. They trace their roots back beyond the agnosticism of Protagoras, whose fifth century B. C. heresy stunned his Athenian compatriots: "As to the gods, I have no way of knowing whether they exist or do not exist." "Man is the measure of all things." Rather, today's secularists find inspiration in the contemptuous questions and prevaricating declarations of the Tempter in Eden: "Has God really said. . . ?" "You surely won't die!" Here is secular humanism at its point of origin: denial of the very authority of God; hence, denial of God's existence and, consequently, denial of eternal accountability to God. "As nontheists," says the 1973 *Humanist Manifesto II*, "we begin with humans, not God, nature not deity."

The corollary to secular humanism's denial of God's existence and authority and of humanity's accountability becomes human autonomy. Erich Fromm has written that the ethics of humanism "is based on the principle that only man himself can determine the criterion for virtue and sin, and not an authority transcending him." One scarcely needs to be a pessimist about the human condition to understand how quickly self-interest and lust for power "determine the criterion" for right and wrong, leading inevitably toward solipsism and the justification of one's own behavior for one's own best reasons. From autonomy the slide toward an abyss called anarchy is precipitous and swift. How, then, could a leading evangelical—a consulting editor to the New Scofield Reference Bible, editor of *Our Hope* magazine, coeditor of *Christianity Today*, general editor of *The Expositor's Bible Commentary* based on the New International

Version of the Bible, for which he was chairman of the English style committee—how could he gamble with his reputation and effectiveness as an evangelical spokesman by adopting for himself a term like Christian humanist?

Certainly, Gaebelein affirmed the existence of God, his divine authority as Creator and Judge, and our accountability as human beings, unrighteous because of sin, to find our only righteousness by faith in the redemption offered in Jesus Christ. But Gaebelein was not a man to give up on the English language just because its historic usage had been corrupted by shoddy speech. He would not allow the now-common debasing of the word "gay"—by journalists and broadcasters, by careless common talk—to be wrested from his vocabulary and turned into a reference to homosexuality; he would not allow the word "myth" to become a synonym for "falsehood." Nor would he permit unthinking Christians to ally themselves carelessly with disbelievers who had co-opted the word "humanism" and laid exclusive claim to it.

Instead, as the teacher he had been for half his life, Gaebelein persisted in attempting to instruct and reconstruct, to inform and reform, Christians whose language usage revealed a lack of knowledge or an impoverished discernment. He would not concede to ignorance; he would not insult the Christian community by pandering to its own preferred cliches and shibboleths. So his lectures at seminaries and colleges, his essays and articles in evangelical magazines, continued to strike the same theme first enunciated in his Griffith Thomas Memorial Lectures at Dallas Theological Seminary in 1952, later published as *The Pattern of God's Truth* (Oxford University Press):

> Truth, though it comprehends finite things, is greater than all it comprehends: its only limitation is the acceptance of its opposite, which is error. And though it includes the finite, it has also its infinite dimensions, because it inheres in the very nature of God Himself. For Christian education, therefore, to adopt as its unifying principle Christ and the Bible means

nothing short of the recognition that *all truth is God's truth*. . . .

It is no accident that St. Paul, setting before the Philippian church a charter for Christian thought, wrote: "Finally, brethren, whatsoever things are true . . . think on these things." He knew that Christian truth embraces all truth, and that nothing true is outside the scope of Christianity.

PHIL 4:8

By "Christian humanist," therefore, Gaebelein meant to identify with believers throughout the ages, particularly those in the fourteenth to seventeenth centuries in northern Europe—Christians such as Petrarch, Michelangelo, Dante, Wycliffe, Tyndale, Thomas More, Luther, Melanchthon, Calvin, Erasmus, Lancelot Andrewes, Donne, Milton, whose love of God found expression in their human gifts and talents as poet, musician, painter, scholar, preacher, statesman. These were *humanists* in the best sense of the word: human beings committed to living out their sojourn on this earth in the fullest possible realization of their attributes as creatures made in the image of God. They were *Christian* humanists inasmuch as they claimed the merits of the atoning work of grace at Calvary, by which their human experience took on its preparation for eternal life in the presence of God. As headmaster of The Stony Brook School, Gaebelein once asked a young English teacher about the play currently under study in a tenth grade class, *Our Town* by Thornton Wilder. A bit of dialogue came into the discussion, the question Emily Webb asks the Stage Manager following her brief return to life in the village of Grovers Corners:

> *Emily*: Do any human beings ever realize life while they live it?—every, every minute?
> *Stage Manager*: No. [Pause] The saints and poets, maybe—they do some.

"There you have it!" the headmaster exclaimed, "a working definition of Christian humanism!"

The revival of a truly Christian humanism was never far

from Gaebelein's central concerns. In a note to himself—one of hundreds found among his papers—dating from around 1975, he wrote:

> Why, when everything from transcendental medita-
> tion at $100 per lesson to astrology has a hearing—
> not an authentic Christian humanism? Christian
> humanism, such as Bush describes, is not a museum
> piece. It is a living option, a necessary alternative
> today. And humanism had and has its eminent prac-
> titioners, like C. S. Lewis, Tolkien, Sayers, Edmund
> Fuller, Chad Walsh, Thomas Howard.

Gaebelein's mention of Douglas Bush refers to a citation in *The Renaissance and English Humanism*, quoting Desiderius Erasmus, "All studies, philosophy, rhetoric are followed for this one object, that we may know Christ and honor Him. This is the end of all learning and eloquence." For Frank E. Gaebelein, as for Erasmus, the "one object" remained the same: knowing Christ and honoring him.

* * *

The roots of Frank Gaebelein's Christian humanism may be found in his childhood. Born on 31 March 1899, in Mount Vernon, New York, he grew up in a God-fearing home, the youngest son of Arno Clemens Gaebelein and his wife Emma. Arno C. Gaebelein had emigrated to America from his native Thuringia, Germany, at age eighteen. His formal schooling had ended in the German *Gymnasium* or high school, but his interest in learning had never flagged. Even without the advantages of formal higher education, Arno C. Gaebelein became known as a biblical scholar; a linguist competent in Greek, Hebrew, Aramaic, Arabic, Syriac, and other Semitic languages; a trans-lator; a teacher and preacher of profound insight; author of more than fifty books, including the multivolume *Annotated Bible*; one of the original editors of the Scofield Reference Bible;

editor of *Our Hope* magazine and of its related publishing house for more than fifty years. Add to all these responsibilities his annual itinerary, before air travel became common, of some fifty thousand miles to fulfill his many speaking engagements, and one has some description of an indefatigable man!

Arno C. Gaebelein had committed himself in service to his Lord in 1879, soon after arriving in America. Working at a woolen mill in Lawrence, Massachusetts, he found spiritual fellowship among an emigrant congregation of German Methodists, where he served his apprenticeship as a Sunday school teacher and church visitor, receiving his license to preach in 1880. In 1884, Gaebelein became pastor of a Methodist church in Harlem. There he met and married the daughter of a leading Methodist minister. In Emma Grimm, Gaebelein found a wife wholly supportive and able to complement his own attributes.

Both as a young pastor and later as a man of many pressing responsibilities, Arno Gaebelein would occasionally feel a twinge of guilt concerning his need to be more hospitable. His son Frank used to recall with wry humor the consequences of his father's bursts of sociability. "Father would suggest to my mother that this or that particular colleague or neighbor should be invited for dinner," said Frank Gaebelein. "Mother would comply and set a date." Then, according to the younger Gaebelein's account, midway through the meal the host would regret his decision; with no aplomb at all, Arno Gaebelein would simply push back his chair from the table, announcing to guests and family alike, "I go to my study."

But Arno Gaebelein did take time to enjoy his family and his love of God's wonders in nature. "Next to God's Word," he wrote in his autobiography, *Half a Century*, "I love to study His other great Book, where He has revealed Himself and where He speaks to our heart—Nature. I love the beautiful!" According to Wilbur M. Smith, Arno Gaebelein was a man well acquainted with the out-of-doors:

He was a superb walker and tramped many miles, alone and with his sons, in the White Mountains and in the Catskills. . . . His knowledge of trees, flowers, and herbs was remarkable, extending even to accurate use of the scientific botanical terminology.

For Frank Gaebelein and his two older brothers, Paul Whitefield and Arno Wesley—a sister Claudia had died in infancy—their home also was a place of joy found in diversion and recreation. Both Arno and Emma Gaebelein loved music. While not a performing pianist, Arno Gaebelein could hold his own in four-hand piano duets. One of Frank Gaebelein's earliest recollections was that of watching and listening to his father and elder brother Paul playing together. Some time later, little Frank went to the piano to pick out a melody by ear. At last he found the right keys, and to help him succeed more swiftly the next time, he gouged a mark in the wood above the starting note. Needless to say, his father took this as a sign that the child was eager for piano lessons, which began soon thereafter. His mother also recognized her youngest son's fascination with the piano and made a point of taking him to concerts and recitals. The experience, in 1908, of hearing the Polish virtuoso Ignace Paderewski perform at Carnegie Hall transported the nine-year-old boy. He never ceased to revere his mother for what she had given him, and his childhood acquaintance with great music at first hand influenced his later attitudes toward music in education.

Throughout his school years and on into university, Frank Gaebelein continued his piano studies, presumably toward a career as a professional musician, perhaps even a pianist like those he heard in the great music halls. At New York University's campus in the Bronx, where he enrolled after graduating from Mount Vernon High School, Gaebelein entered fully into undergraduate musical activities. He accompanied the glee club, performing as soloist in concerts. But by this time, other interests were also beginning to show themselves. For instance, at Mount Vernon High School Gaebelein had been editor of the yearbook, assisted by a friend named E. B. White, who would become the great essayist and humorist for *The New Yorker*. Now at New York University, Gaebelein continued his writing, adding the campus newspaper to his college yearbook experience. He also joined the track team, then trained by the redoubtable Emil von Elling, one of America's premier coaches. Tall and strong, Gaebelein was a quartermiler running for the Violet in the Millrose Games and at the Penn Relays. With all these activities, Gaebelein nonetheless retained his academic purpose and, in 1920, received his bachelor of arts degree in English, with election to Phi Beta Kappa.

During this period of maturing from boy to young manhood, Gaebelein was also coming under two other influences, his love of mountains and his growing relationship with Jesus Christ. As with so many persons of spiritual depth and vision, Gaebelein's appreciation of mountain ranges became for him an illustration of the majesty and supremacy of God's creation.

Arno Gaebelein had been invited to preach at the First Presbyterian Church of Colorado Springs, Colorado; his family accompanied him on the train. For the boy Frank Gaebelein, his first sight of the Rockies created an indelible image of grandeur, an image to which he would return again and again in his writing and speaking; an image he came eventually to know at firsthand as he acquired the skills and experience of technical mountaineering. One of his earliest climbs was Mount Hood, near Portland, Oregon; over the rest of his life, he climbed in Switzerland, Iceland, Mexico, and Canada, where his beloved Canadian Rockies never ceased to thrill him. Among his proudest moments was the opportunity, atop a peak in the French Alps, to pause with his guide, the renowned alpinist Lionel Terray, to read from the French New Testament and offer prayers of thanksgiving. Gaebelein's sermons preached before comrades in climbing and published in the journals of the American and Canadian Alpine clubs gave witness not only to his love of mountains but also his love for the Creator of such magnificence.

This personal relationship with God had grown out of a childhood faith nurtured by his godly parents. Unlike the stereotype of a German family, Arno and Emma Gaebelein's home exuded loving respect, not Prussian authoritarianism. Young Frank and his brothers were never cowed into religious observance. Instead, their parents lived before them in such a way that faith in Jesus Christ took on immediacy and the unmistakable ring of truth. "Our home was a Christian home," Frank Gaebelein said, "not because my father was a noted preacher or because my mother was constantly talking to my brothers and me about Christianity, but because of the good sense with which they lived their faith. They never told me to read the Bible; yet I began to do so very early. I'm sure I learned to give some part of each day to the Scriptures from seeing my father and mother do so."

His habit of daily Bible reading and prayer shaped Gaebelein's character. From regular study of the Scriptures he obtained his biblical frame of reference; from daily periods of prayer, he found the fortitude and encouragement to sustain his faith. His reading was never perfunctory, his intercessory prayers never merely ritual. He read the Scriptures expecting to find new insight into its truths; he prayed in quite specific ways for specific persons and their needs. Throughout his more than four decades as headmaster at Stony Brook, Gaebelein prayed daily for each student and faculty member by name. He also maintained a file of hundreds of very personal prayers, many of them written on three-by-five cards. "Why written prayers?" he asked rhetorically in a letter of 22 February 1981.

> Because in times of need or special stress I've written prayers as a way of concentrating my petitions. Some people have had, I think, an unrealistic view of my prayer-life. But I've had my struggles with rote prayer, merely dutiful prayer, wandering thoughts, and all that. And I've found at times that writing prayers has helped me concentrate on the Lord.

"The prayers were not written for publication," he wrote, adamantly underscoring his words. "I've kept them because at times it's been an encouragement to look back and see how the Lord has dealt with them."

A personal instance comes to mind as an illustration. In January 1961, our daughter Ellyn, then only an infant of three months, appeared close to death because of staphylococcus infection. Several times during her hospitalization, Gaebelein came to our dormitory apartment on the campus of The Stony Brook School to pray with Lory and me. Then one evening, at the height of our baby's crisis, he called me to his study in Grosvenor House, the headmaster's residence. There he showed me two packets of file cards each bound by rubber bands. "I often write prayers for particular needs," he told me. "When the Lord chooses to answer these prayers, I move my written prayer from this pile to that. But I keep the record of my answered prayers as a means of thanksgiving."

Looking at me with those deeply piercing eyes and placing his hand on my shoulder with the force of a loving mentor, Gaebelein said, "Bruce, I want you to know that I've just moved my prayer for your daughter's well-being from this pile of requests to that pile of answered prayers." Then he led us in a prayer of thanksgiving.

From that evening on, my wife and I believed that God would restore our baby's health, a fact confirmed by our next morning's call from the pediatrician.

Gaebelein loved the Bible and revered it as God's written revelation of truth. But he did not treat it as a magic book, and he did not subscribe to the opinion prevalent among many Christians in the middle of this century that only the King James Version could be read and believed as the authentic Word of God. His view of inspiration tolerated no chauvinism nor provincialism. "What do French or Chinese Christians read?" he would ask impatiently. So, while he treasured the literary merits of the King James Version, he was also vice-chairman of the committee of evangelical scholars who, in 1967, revised and published the New Scofield Reference Bible, a revision that rendered the King James text in a more readable fashion for today's audience. Soon thereafter, Gaebelein accepted responsibility to serve as chairman of the English Style Committee of the New International Version, seeking clarity and felicity of language for the text of this new Bible, published in 1978.

Furthermore, Gaebelein never became embroiled in the current inerrancy controversy—just as, many years before, he had risen above the separatist-vs.-ecumenist conflict by serving on the organizing committee for Billy Graham's 1957 Madison Square Garden crusade. While he maintained unflinchingly that the Scriptures are God's divinely inspired Word—God's truth expressed in language—Gaebelein deplored the excesses by some proponents of textual inerrancy. To him their argument, however well intentioned, stood on the flimsiest stilts as a *reductio ad absurdum*. Without the original manuscripts, how could one *prove* that their authors had been free from error? Was not a greater act of faith required to trust in a God who, by his very nature, is Truth, whose Word must therefore also be Truth? Is not the fact that the Scriptures have been preserved at all, in the face of great hostility and deliberate attempts to rid the world of the Bible, sufficient evidence of the Scriptures' divine and inerrant authority?

Instead of tilting at windmills, Frank Gaebelein preferred to read and study and teach the Bible as given to him—his French-language New Testament, the Jerusalem Bible he greatly admired, the NIV of which he was so much an advocate, or the familiar King James Version which he called "this beloved and beautiful translation"—confident that the Holy Spirit was the guardian and ultimate revealer of truth. From such reading, study, and teaching, Gaebelein expected a Christian world-and-life-view to be formulated. He lamented the fact, however, that too few Christians took as their obligation the development of such a world-and-life-view. In *The Pattern of God's Truth* he wrote:

It is a sad fact that the Protestant principle of the competence of the individual believer to interpret the Bible under the guidance of the Spirit is so frequently honored only in the breach. Many Christians today are notoriously lazy-minded. Too often the Protestant layman relies solely upon his minister for the understanding and, if the truth be told, even for the reading of his Bible. Such secondhand acquaintance with God's Word can never form a man's thinking upon revelational lines. Even among evangelicals who read the Bible and attend Bible conferences as well as church, there is an excess of reliance upon what other men say about the Word of God instead of upon what it says directly to the individual. In all honesty, it must be admitted that no teacher or minister who does not have the Bible at the center of his life and thought to the extent of living daily in this book can hope to develop a Christian frame of reference.

From childhood, therefore, throughout his long life, Frank Gaebelein remained a student of Scripture. Like his father, he had no formal theological or seminary education. Instead, upon his graduation from New York University, he enrolled at Harvard University, studying English and comparative literature. Among his teachers were the famous critics John Livingston Lowes and Irving Babbitt, from whom, unquestionably, Gaebelein received his first formal introduction to the subject of aesthetics. A vigorous opponent of modern naturalism in literature, with its fascination for the basest elements of human experience, Babbitt championed instead the classic virtues of truth and beauty to be found in nature and in human nature.

But by far the most important teacher in Gaebelein's year at Harvard, if not the most influential in all his schooling, was Dean L. B. R. Briggs. In spite of his several administrative and scholarly responsibilities, Dean Briggs insisted upon teaching a writing seminar. There he encountered Frank Gaebelein—brilliant, eager to learn, his prematurely balding and aquiline features giving him an appearance of scholarly intensity. Gaebelein's artistic temperament had lent itself to expression in prose his previous teachers had often praised, commending his tendency toward flowery language. Dean Briggs held quite an opposite view, disdaining "ease and elegance" for a style stripped of excessive adjectives, strongly dependent upon concrete nouns and verbs in the active voice. In short, Briggs tore away at Gaebelein's florid circumlocutions, demanding directness and clarity, precision and reliance upon the starkness of the unadorned noun and evocative verb to do their work in a reader's imagination. From Dean Briggs, Gaebelein learned a new style, whose beauty lies in its very simplicity.

And what of Gaebelein's music and his early aspirations to become a concert pianist? Although he continued to play and even to perform, certain circumstances through which may be read the providence of God had arisen to alter the course of his life. Early in 1918, while still enrolled at New York University, Gaebelein had enlisted in the officer training program, passed the qualifying standards, and been commissioned as a second lieutenant in the United States Army. He left the college campus to become an infantry training officer at the Plattsburgh Barracks Training Camp in northern New York state. There he remained until November 1918, when the war to end all wars came to an armistice. Upon his return to New York University, Gaebelein discovered that he no longer viewed life exclusively through the eyes of a would-be professional musician. Instead, he had found another art—writing and literature—to share with music, a decision he was wise enough to realize would mean the end of any career as a musician, for music is a jealous mistress and shares her place with no other.

Yet music would always be close to Gaebelein's heart. So when, much to his surprise, even dismay, he learned that Dean Briggs had nominated him for one of Harvard's commencement addresses by students from its several divisions, Gaebelein chose to write his remarks "In Behalf of Music." Gaebelein's essay was selected, and he was informed that he would represent the graduate school at the commencement exercises on 23 June 1921. Not only must he speak before a crowd in Sanders Theatre, but his speech must be memorized. To Frank Gaebelein, bashful and hampered by a speech impediment, this announcement struck like a dead weight. He believed that he could not possibly comply and sought out Dean Briggs to withdraw. But Briggs would not hear of such nonsense! Of course Gaebelein would speak, and Dean Briggs would help to prepare him for the public occasion himself.

> He told me to meet him in Sanders Theatre rather late one night and put me behind the lectern, then told me to begin my remarks. I could hardly see him in the dimness of that auditorium, but I knew that he was moving from place to place, calling out useful and constructive criticism to me. Once I recognized his voice all the way from the back row of the balcony. He made me repeat the entire speech several times, after each delivery offering some word of helpful instruction. I could feel my confidence growing. By the time those fearful exercises came, I was ready to speak.

Thus whole generations of students at The Stony Brook School, congregations in churches throughout North America, and audiences at colleges, seminaries, and conferences owe to a Harvard dean the eloquence and persuasive power of the preacher and lecturer Frank E. Gaebelein was to become.

The text of Gaebelein's earliest public address, which appears elsewhere in this anthology, is more than a piece of juvenilia. Young though he was, Gaebelein nonetheless possessed a serious and probing mind; he would never have been content with what he called, in this same speech, "a skimming of surfaces, a mere dilettantism." Into his brief remarks, taking only ten minutes or so, he managed to compress a far-ranging critique of modern society's ignorance of music, compounded by a lack of regret over such ignorance. His point, succinctly stated, was this: "Is not a little understanding of music as essential to a truly liberal education as chemical theories or trigonometry?"

Furthermore, Gaebelein made certain that his audience could be in no doubt as to the vantage from which he spoke. His was not the argument of some artistic elitist, some cultural snob, some unreconstructed classicist. Rather, he grounded his case upon the words of Scripture, near the end of his speech quoting from Paul:

> What is needed now . . . is a renaissance of music among all of the educated. For, just as much as poetry and the drama, music is universal property. It is not for the musician alone; it is for all who lay claim to knowledge. It is one of those things which Saint Paul exhorts us to "think on"—the true, the honest, the pure, the lovely, and the "things of good report."

Throughout his long career, Frank Gaebelein kept before him another challenge from the apostle Paul: "I am not ashamed of the gospel." Wherever he went—as a Christian educator attending a convention of independent schools or a meeting of fellow-headmasters; as a Christian who played the piano or climbed mountains; as a Christian active in the affairs of his prestigious Cosmos Club in Washington, D. C.—Gaebelein refused to hide his light under a bushel. He was not obnoxious about his witness for Jesus Christ; he simply would not sit back quietly and allow presumably educated persons to make uninformed statements about matters of utmost importance to a Christian. So too he urged his faculty at Stony Brook to be staunch and bold in the face of academic hostility toward the Christian faith. "Let them know where you stand," he would exhort the faculty, "especially those who teach in schools that owe their very existence to believing Christian founders." How interesting to note that, even as a young man, Frank Gaebelein was not ashamed to quote the Bible at Harvard University.

By 23 June 1921, the date of the Harvard commencement address, Gaebelein had already agreed to serve as founding headmaster of a school for boys, to be situated on the grounds of the Stony Brook Assembly at Stony Brook, Long Island. The Stony Brook Assembly, founded in 1907 by an interdenominational committee of pastors and Christian laymen, had been conducting summer conferences since 1909. A handsome auditorium, built on a design similar to the Billy Sunday tabernacles, could hold a thousand and more listeners to some of the great preachers of the day—F. B. Meyer, J. Wilbur Chapman, G. Campbell Morgan, Maitland Alexander, and Arno C. Gaebelein, among others. Two summer hotels had been constructed to replace the tents that once dotted the grounds, and many permanent cottages and larger residences were being built by permanent investors in the Stony Brook Assembly.

The president of the Assembly and its visionary was John Fleming Carson, pastor of Central Presbyterian Church, Brooklyn, New York, and the 1911 moderator of the General Assembly of the Presbyterian Church in the U. S. A. From the Assembly's earliest days, Carson had hoped to emulate Dwight L. Moody, whose conferences at Northfield, Massachusetts, led to the founding of his Northfield and Mount Hermon schools for girls and boys. Three years after the armistice, Carson was ready to launch the school. But who should lead such a venture? Carson's coworker in the Stony Brook Assembly, Ford C. Ottman, suggested that Carson consider the son of their mutual friend, Arno Gaebelein.

Shortly after his twenty-second birthday, Frank Gaebelein received an invitation to travel from Cambridge to New York City for a luncheon meeting with Carson and Ottman. Over their meal, the three men discussed the plans for the intended founding of a new school—wholly abstractly, so Gaebelein assumed. "I was rather naive, I suppose," said Gaebelein, "not to realize what they were getting at. But the idea of my entering upon such a venture as they proposed never crossed my mind. After all, I had no interest in secondary education; I was considering several possibilities in college teaching." At some point in the discussion, Carson and Ottman unceremoniously excused them-selves from the table to take up a private conversation just out of their guest's earshot. When they returned to the table, Carson made an offer on behalf of the Stony Brook Assembly: Would Frank Gaebelein accept the position of principal (later the title was changed to headmaster) of The Stony Brook School?

Gaebelein was dumbfounded. Apart from his own school-ing at Mount Vernon High School, he had no experience what-ever in secondary education. "I was not a preparatory school graduate," he recalled. "In fact, although my father had often preached in the auditorium at Stony Brook, I had never been on the grounds myself; nor had I ever visited the campus of such a school as I was to help to found." Yet something about the oppor-tunity presented to him appealed to this unusual young man. He promised to consider prayerfully its challenge and returned to Cambridge, his mind a maelstrom of doubts and hopes. Over the next few days of prayer and carefully weighed advice, Gaebelein made a historic decision so far as American education and Christian schooling in particular are concerned. He ac-cepted the challenge to head a school, as yet in name only—no faculty, no students, no curriculum, no funds—hoping to begin classes in the fall of 1922. He began work in September 1921, with only twelve months in which to develop a constituency willing to support such a risky venture, parents willing to trust their sons to a fledgling school and its inexperienced administra-tor, not to mention teachers of sufficient faith to believe that they were not jeopardizing their families and careers by signing on with such a novice.

The philosophical cast of mind marking the young Har-vard graduate found its ready application in the preliminary planning for the school that was to be. Installed in an office in the Presbyterian Building in New York City, Gaebelein's first official business was to draft a publication announcing The Stony Brook School. He wasted no time in establishing the new school's intentions to stand "outside the modern trend." This trend he took to be an opposition to orthodox Christianity throughout American education, secondary and higher. Instead of writing off spiritual regeneration "on psychological grounds" or tampering with "the doctrine of the Deity of our Lord" or offering religious instruction "perfunctory and of slender value," Stony Brook intended

> to give accurate teaching upon the Christianity of the Bible and to demonstrate that this teaching belongs of right with thorough scholarship and sound education.

A little wordy (Dean Briggs might have cautioned), but at least Gaebelein's brochure made its point. Furthermore, the new principal went on, to bring about such an education,

> classical studies will not be discarded for those subjects the value of which is entirely practical. A truly successful education must build up the foundations of a mental and spiritual background, and, for accomplishing this, humanistic studies are invaluable. In combining with them Christian truth and the glorious literature of the English Bible, the school has an instrument two-edged and of high cultural value.

From his earliest days as an educational thinker, Gaebelein gave highest priority to instruction in the Bible as the essential complement of a liberal arts or humanities education. Indeed, the Bible would take its place at the center of Stony Brook's curriculum. During the course of his planning year, Gaebelein visited many established preparatory schools, most of which included the teaching of religious studies in their programs. But nowhere did he find a model for what he was proposing. At the famed Lawrenceville School, for example, Gaebelein spoke with Mather Abbott, a legend among schoolmen. "Bot," as he was known, taught a course to seniors called Bible, but his own biographer records that on the first day of school, when a newly arrived student appeared at the headmaster's classroom door carrying a copy of the Bible, "Bot" roared at him, "You won't need that here!" Several years after the founding of The Stony Brook School, Mather Abbott recalled for an interviewer from *The Christian Science Monitor* his meeting with young Frank Gaebelein:

> He came with his youthful enthusiasm, telling me that he was going to make the Bible the major study and teach it three times a week, and I was tremendously impressed. I said to myself as he sat there, "Would that I were he! Is it possible? Can he do it?" Well, he seems to have done it. I would that I could teach the Bible that often in my school, but I cannot have it more than once a week. I do not believe there is another school in the country that is doing it. It takes courage to put spiritual things first nowadays.

The Bible remained at the forefront of Gaebelein's work both as an educator and as a writer. Most of the fourteen books he wrote are specifically addressed to topics about the Bible— *Down Through the Ages*; *A Brief Survey of Scripture*; *Exploring the Bible*; *Facing the Fact of Inspiration*; *Philemon: The Gospel of Emancipation*; *Looking Unto Him*; *The Christian Use of the Bible*; *The Servant and the Dove*; *The Practical Epistle of James*. At his death, Gaebelein was busy with the enormous duties of editing for Zondervan Publishing House the series of commentaries on the NIV text.

The school opened on 13 September 1922, with ceremonies vastly more impressive than a student body of twenty-seven boys and eight teachers might have warranted. Hundreds of people, including dignitaries from academic life, politics, commerce, and the church were present. Two major addresses highlighted the event, the first by the young schoolman. His ambitious title was "The Plan and Scope of Stony Brook School." To begin, Gaebelein discounted the idea that Stony Brook was "an experiment as experiments are popularly conceived." Rather, he said, this school was to be "an enterprise built upon the foundational truths of Christianity." He went on:

These are the great and abiding things—the eternal verities. Our contemporary philosophy, a large part of our religious thought, is colored by the idea of relativism, the endless ebb and flow of things. Yet the great truths remain. They are immutable, abiding— as much more firmly fixed than the mountains as the infinite transcends the finite. They cannot be shaken; they constitute "the everlasting yea."

It is upon this rock that The Stony Brook School rests. And it is upon this rock that its future growth will be built.

Early in his address, Gaebelein touched a theme that would mark his contribution to education and to aesthetics for the next sixty years. He spoke of "correlation"; later, he would use the term "integration" and call for an integration of faith, living, and learning. But with remarkable prescience, the twenty-three-year-old headmaster declared that "the central aim of this school is to correlate Christian principles, the great and eternal verities, with education of a type high enough to merit intimacy with such exalted ideals." Since the entire address appears in this collection, no further synopsis is necessary, except to point out that, as the peroration to his remarks, Gaebelein once more sounded his call for an unqualified Christian humanism:

> In order to put these principles into practice in the most efficient way possible, the Christian school must be humanistic in the best sense of the word. For the Christian point of view is itself in essence humanistic. The fatal misconception of the scholastics of the middle ages, that Christianity is incompatible with liberal education, ought never to be revived. The greatest injury that the Christian institution can render to its faith is to fall, at this late day, into obscurantism. A humanism that would have every essential study taught in the most efficient way

possible, that would never yield one jot in the field of scholarship; a humanism that, in its broad application, would help each individual student to solve his own unique intellectual and spiritual problems—this will guide the faculty of the Stony Brook School in their glorious adventure in Christian education—an adventure that will serve the Church of Jesus Christ by conserving the faith of her youth, an adventure that will serve the nation by giving to it, year by year, a body of young men of stalwart character, well-taught and nurtured in the faith.

The second address by the presumed main speaker for the occasion was almost anticlimactic. Francis L. Patton, former president of Princeton University, then president of Princeton Theological Seminary, called for "the Fourth R" in education—religion to accompany reading, 'riting, and 'rithmetic. But a more piercing clarion had already sounded; the audience present at Stony Brook that day—and those who read Frank Gaebelein's address in its published form—realized that a young prophet had been raised up in their midst. By the time he retired as headmaster of The Stony Brook School, in 1963, he had built—by God's grace and providence, as he would be quick to say—a school unique in all America for its unwavering witness for Jesus Christ through a rigorous college-preparatory curriculum in the liberal arts. In every respect, Gaebelein had accomplished his goal of reestablishing a base for a revival of Christian humanism.

Undoubtedly the greatest single human influence in Gaebelein's life was his wife, Dorothy Medd Gaebelein, whom he married midway through the second year of the school's existence. For almost fifty-seven years, until her passing in 1980, Mrs. Gaebelein was her husband's companion and support. A Vassar graduate, well-bred, refined, utterly gracious, Dorothy Gaebelein was also efficiently practical in ways her husband's genius could hardly approach. For instance, he was a most frightful driver; one trembled at the thought of his offer to transport his guest back and forth from the airport. His wife, on the other hand, drove with skill to match her considerable speed. Like many great men, Gaebelein's concentration upon the highest ideal could at times miss some minuscule detail distracting to others. His wife stood by, however, to prevent or at least limit such distractions as much as possible. For instance, she presided over formal occasions, such as weddings in the Stony Brook chapel, forbidding by the very force of her presence intrusive photographers from turning a sacred ceremony into a spectacle.

With the help of her sister Miriam Medd, Dorothy Gaebelein transformed the campus of The Stony Brook School from a semibarren meadow into a veritable arboretum of plants, shrubs, and trees of all descriptions, colors, and seasons. She placed flowering shrubs in arrangements so that, as their annual blossoms appeared, the grounds of the school took on the appearance of a well-ordered garden. She encouraged the planting of unusual trees—even rare for Long Island—such as the great Rose Margin beech, now standing guard over the chapel. The birth of each of her children she marked by planting a Colorado blue spruce. A European larch, a Japanese umbrella pine, a gingko tree, and a cedar of Lebanon hybrid were among some of the others she planted. Under her careful eye, the campus became her canvas, her loom, on which she painted and wove a thing of beauty.

What she did on the campus Dorothy Gaebelein also brought to Grosvenor House, the headmaster's home. She hung on its walls paintings and watercolors of distinction, some by Paul King, a Stony Brook neighbor, as well as the etchings and drawings of Grant Reynard, another friend. Far from wealthy, the Gaebeleins nonetheless knew the value of fine works of art. Together they acquired selectively such paintings as might bring joy to their home. They bought only works of quality for the same reason that Frank Gaebelein seldom wasted his time listening to popular music: he wanted to surround himself with art that would last.

Frank and Dorothy Gaebelein's home life differed to some degree from the usual because they lived in the whirl of a boarding school ten months out of each year. In the summers the Stony Brook Assembly brought conference guests and speakers into their lives. Yet these parents worked together to shield their children—Dorothy, Donn, and Gretchen—from the effects of limited privacy and a busy father's hectic schedule. The Gaebelein children were brought up in the same spirit that had pervaded their father's home in Mount Vernon. Although conscious of the do's and don'ts of their evangelical constituency, Frank and Dorothy Gaebelein were free from the banality of legalism itself. Instead of fundamentalism's austere taboos, their children were introduced to the blessings of God's common grace mediated through the arts. Others might listen to the radio and hear "The Longines Symphonette" broadcasting classical music; the Gaebelein children had met Michel Piastro, concertmaster of the New York Philharmonic, who brought his radio ensemble to play at Stony Brook. Others might study music history in school; these children knew their father's friend, Clarence Adler, whose own teacher had been taught by Franz Liszt, and they had seen Dr. Adler and their father perform duo-piano concertos in concert. They also knew their father's student in senior Bible class, a young Cuban virtuoso named Jorge Bolet, one of today's giants of the keyboard, who offered a memorial recital in Frank Gaebelein's honor the day after his death in 1983.

For their own part, the Gaebelein children had their opportunities to study the piano. Both girls seemed to enjoy lessons; young Donn endured for four years. "I was awful," he says, "didn't like it, and fought it. Finally, my teacher kindly advised my folks that it was a waste of time and money. They never pushed it further." The Gaebeleins had a phonograph on which recordings were played, and the radio was often tuned to broadcasts of Walter Damrosch's New York Philharmonic. The children accompanied their parents to concerts in Carson Auditorium on the school campus—for many years, the main cultural site and concert hall on Long Island's North Shore. But, Donn Gaebelein recalls, "as I grew up, Dad was the main source of music in our house. I enjoyed going to sleep hearing beautiful music as he practiced." Mrs. Gaebelein would call from another part of the house, "Frank, that is beautiful."

Each Sunday evening during the academic year, the Gaebeleins entertained students. These were times when the headmaster seemed much less stern and forbidding as he sat at his piano, talking with his youthful audience about the piece he was to play, illustrating his lesson, sometimes sharing the keyboard in a duet with a talented pupil. Through such experiences, along with the regular series of recitals and concerts he scheduled for the school, Gaebelein obtained his working theory on teaching music and his corollary bias against traditional courses in music appreciation. Music must be heard to be enjoyed, and it must be heard in performance by authentic musicians; furthermore, he maintained, one live concert is worth a whole semester of recordings in a music classroom. Perhaps this is why, in his four decades as headmaster, he rarely had a full-time teacher of music on the faculty. A notable exception was the distinguished baritone soloist, Frank Boggs, who taught and directed choral music at Stony Brook in the midfifties. Today Frank Boggs is director of music at The Westminster Schools of Atlanta, Georgia, where Donn Medd Gaebelein is president.

During the Sunday evening entertainments, Frank Gaebelein also offered another art form to the boys who attended. He would read aloud from some of the literature he loved—a long narrative poem, a mystery story, a humorous dialect tale, or part of a novel. He read with all the voices distinct and identifiable, and he read with obvious pleasure in sharing the text with his students, as well as his own three children, who regularly attended as they chose. "Dad loved to read," says his son. "He never missed a chance to read to us as adults, whenever he visited our homes or on a trip together somewhere." The art of narrative, the art of fiction, the art of literature—these too were close to Gaebelein's heart.

On all these occasions—as well as at the weekly Tuesday night fellowship for prayer and Bible study, which convened voluntarily in the Gaebelein home—Dorothy remained in the background, preparing snacks and beverage for always grateful boys. She saw herself as her husband's helper, unobtrusively serving his needs and the wants of the teenage boys who crowded into the living room of Grosvenor House. She knew them all by name; their birthdays were duly commemorated; some sought her special kind of counsel. But for the most part, she did her work quietly and without drawing attention to herself. As the school's enrollment grew, so too her influence expanded, particularly in her informal teaching of the social graces. A boys' school can be a den of adolescent barbarians, if left on their own, but Mrs. Gaebelein exerted a civilizing effect upon most of them. She insisted upon courtesy, manners, decorum, although never at the expense of good humor. She also exercised her quiet authority and example on members of the faculty and their wives. Often young themselves, these couples naturally looked to the headmaster and his wife to set the tone for domestic as well as institutional matters. Dorothy Gaebelein's example did not pass unnoticed. Along with unflagging hospitality to students and faculty and unswerving loyalty to her husband's calling, her good taste has been her great legacy to Stony Brook.

Her husband knew the worth of her contribution and spoke of her work from time to time; yet in the manner of self-effacing spouses, she always appeared to temper his mention of her part with an offhand remark. Later, following retirement from Stony Brook to the active life of Washington, D. C., Gaebelein seemed to feel more at ease in speaking of his wife's support during his forty-one years as headmaster. On the occasion of his eightieth birthday, 31 March 1979, a group of long-term Stony Brook people journeyed to Arlington, Virginia, for a luncheon celebration. But Mrs. Gaebelein was too sick to attend. It was then Frank Gaebelein opened his soul to the men and women with whom he had worked at Stony Brook, lovingly recalling how dependent he had always been upon his dear Dorothy.

Her death, eighteen months later, meant a staggeringly painful separation, however temporary the devout may claim. Frank Gaebelein now spoke increasingly of what she had meant in his life. The final conversation we had was a telephone call to a seminary where I was about to give a lecture; in fact, I delayed going onto the platform when summoned to the phone. Gaebelein had entered the hospital that morning for cardiac surgery and was calling from his room. His voice seemed filled with urgency. "I don't know what the outcome of this surgery will be," he said, "but if the Lord wills to take me to himself, I must tell you once more with fervor that all I have ever been able to accomplish has been under God and because of my wife's encouragement. People must know how significant a part she had in all my work."

* * *

The breadth of Frank E. Gaebelein's intellectual scope seems daunting to those of us not blessed with his gifts. The fact that he was a theologian and biblical scholar of sufficient standing to be offered the presidency of leading seminaries doubles in significance when we remember that he was almost wholly self-taught. True, he had his father's influence to rely upon, but Gaebelein's ordination as deacon, then presbyter, in the Reformed Episcopal Church, as well as his endowed seminary lectureships, came about only because of arduous and disciplined study. This same dedicated study had made him, first, a pianist of sufficient ability to consider a concert career; later, however, when music was no longer anything more than an avocation, Gaebelein could still summon himself to the hard work of practice for a concerto appearance with a local orchestra or even for a national radio network program, hosted by the famous music commentator, Milton Cross. Even in his eighties, he was working at learning to play Liszt's Transcendental Etudes and Beethoven's Opus 111.

To achieve all this while at the same time, for a period of forty-one years, administering a growing school—hiring its faculty, presiding over its daily operation, almost single-handedly soliciting its needed funds, constructing and later embodying its reputation—required not only enormous self-discipline but also that unusual quality we call integrity. Frank Gaebelein possessed this quality, as his daughter, Gretchen Gaebelein Hull, has written, "Long before I knew how to spell the word or even knew what it meant, I realized my father was a man of integrity."

That word *integrity* we often limit to judgments concerning a person's honesty: integrity as truthfulness. Certainly, the meaning is valid, but even beyond such denotation, integrity also refers to wholeness: integrity as a complete, unbroken approach to the understanding of truth. None of us can know everything there is to be known about anything; too few of us, however, know anything at all in wholeness or integrity. Instead, we catch glimpses, we perceive scattered fragments, we piece together bits from here and there, striving like paleontologists to form an imagined whole out of our scraps of information. But Gaebelein was one of those few men in any generation not content to know little and speak much. What he knew—as educator, as mountaineer, as pianist, as connoisseur of the arts—he knew because he had chosen to live out his experience. Hence, he spoke about education as a headmaster and teacher who lived among his students; he spoke of mountains as someone whose hands had been roughened by reaching for the next hold, whose knees had been scraped and bruised. He spoke of music as someone who practiced his instrument; in fact, his son Donn recalls, "He practiced a lot!" Frank Gaebelein was no dilettante, no mere dabbler in the arts. When he sat down at the piano keyboard to perform—whether on the National Broadcasting Company's program, "Music Is My Hobby," or for a group of students in his home on a Sunday evening—he played well because he had committed himself to rehearsing and digesting the music long before.

Gaebelein deplored the pontificating and presumed omniscience of certain evangelical spokesmen who dared to utter pronouncements about the arts in general, music in particular, without sufficient credentials to give their words authenticity. For instance, he did not believe that God could be glorified by wellmeant but inaccurate descriptions of music written in the minor key as tacitly morose or universally depressing. Like C. S. Lewis, Gaebelein found it difficult to suffer fools gladly. He would challenge such a statement with a wealth of illustrations—Bach's "Jesu, Meine Freude" ("Jesus, Priceless Treasure") in C minor, or the Hebrew melody "Leoni" ("The God of Abraham Praise") in F minor—and wait for his opponent to explain himself.

Equally dismaying to him were theological arguments based on extrapolation from a narrow range of subjects—a single work to show the decadence of human depravity. He found little value and much potential harm in simplistic explanations of culture—arbitrary lines above or below which God's redemption might be seen or not seen—dependent solely upon the critic's subjective limitations. He recalled, for instance, an occasion when Hans Rookmaker, the Dutch art historian and associate of Francis Schaeffer, was giving an illustrated lecture and making a point concerning a particular painting and its pivotal importance in the supposed decay of art. Gaebelein, who knew the painting, asked a question or two, suggesting disagreement with Rookmaker's interpretation. A brief dialogue ensued, but when Rookmaker saw that his point remained contested, he said, "That's the way it is," and changed the slide to the next picture.

The essence of Gaebelein's aesthetics was never doctrinaire, his standards of appreciation never dogma-derived. Nor was he bound by purely cultural or social norms, although in music he preferred the classics—Bach, Mozart, Beethoven, Chopin, Liszt, Schubert, Brahms, Mendelssohn. Still he could sit with the legendary jazz pianist Teddy Wilson and find common ground in their discussion of theme-and-variation as a parallel to jazz improvisation.

Gaebelein had no stomach for mere aestheticism, an art-for-art's-sake ecstasy of preciousness. Certainly his aesthetics were more than "religious," as that term is often used to describe the work of Tom Driver, Nathan Scott, and Amos Wilder, among others of a theologically liberal leaning. Lastly, Gaebelein could not be labeled "reformed" in the strictest sense of that designation by followers of Herman Dooyeweerd, Abraham Kuyper, Calvin Seerveld, and Nicholas Wolterstorff. He was too fond of quoting such Roman Catholic artists and aestheticians as Francois Mauriac, Jacques Maritain, and Flannery O'Connor to qualify as an exclusively reformed thinker. What, then, is one to say of Frank E. Gaebelein's view of the arts and their place in Christian experience?

Simply this, that he was an evangelical Christian, committed to the unfolding revelation of truth in the Scriptures. His was a biblical aesthetics, developing over many years of thought and practice. He acquired a cumulative understanding of truth and beauty in art as he came into a fuller appreciation of the doctrine of common grace, both enunciated and depicted in the Bible. Gaebelein never confused art with religious faith, unlike his friend Clarence Adler, for whom music was the only religion. Instead, within the arts Gaebelein found expressions of God's grace, intimations of God's love, glimpses of God's perfection, and illustrations of the Christian hope that, while "now we see but a poor reflection, then we shall see face to face."

He seldom missed an opportunity to state this connection he found between music and faith. For a broadcast over WMCA, a major New York City radio station, in January 1935, Gaebelein's script reads like a sermon. One of his themes in this brief talk, here published for the first time under the title "The Greatest of All Songs," is the pervasiveness of music throughout the Bible. "Few but scholars of the text realize . . . that the returned prodigal heard a symphony, as the Greek literally puts it," he told his listeners. On another broadcast, the NBC network program "Music Is My Hobby," Gaebelein spoke of J. S. Bach's chorale, "Rejoice, All Ye Christians," transcribed for piano by Isidor Philipp, as an expression of "deep and Godlike things."

> Though written in the somber key of F minor, it seems to voice the thoughts of the apostle Paul when he spoke of rejoicing in suffering and glorying in tribulation. Just notice how this chorale rises to a triumphant climax that is consummated with a sudden, joyful, major cadence.

In a far different medium than radio—an unpublished poem found among his papers—Gaebelein describes his feeling for Bach's Chaconne in D minor:

> Firm chords march on with solemn, solid tread
> Unto a cadenced, serious close;
> Half-hidden under somber, minor tones
> Burns white the Faith for which the martyrs bled.

As becomes readily apparent in this collection, Gaebelein's reading spanned an astonishing field of literature. His citations range from Jonathan Edwards to Keith Miller, from Eric Sauer to Jacques Barzun, from Aristotle, Augustine, and Anselm to G. K. Chesterton, C. S. Lewis, and Dorothy L. Sayers. But always throughout these essays runs a thread that leads back to the writer's point of origination, the Bible. In *The Pattern of God's Truth*, Gaebelein chose Pierson Curtis, his longtime friend and colleague at Stony Brook, as an example of the skilled teacher, able to integrate the Scriptures and his subject. Speaking of Curtis, he wrote,

> There is no question of this man's professional competence; when he teaches Shakespeare or Milton, he does so with authority born of long and loving familiarity with their works. And all the time there is another book in which, because he is a devoted Christian, he lives in a sense different from his devotion to the English classics. Not only is his heart in the Bible; through his daily use and constant study of it, the Bible has literally formed his mind. Such a man does not make brief journeys from English literature to the Bible. Despite his constant handling of literature, his true intellectual and spiritual home is in the Word of God.

Frank Gaebelein might here have also been describing himself, for he too found "his true intellectual and spiritual home" in the pages of Scripture.

This fact accounts for the uniqueness of his essays. The

subject of aesthetics is one of the most highly charged and yet elusive topics in human discourse. Aphorisms and bromides abound: *De gustibus non disputandum est* ("Concerning taste, there can be no dispute"); "It's all a matter of taste"; and "Beauty is in the eye of the beholder." Obviously, each aesthetician, each evaluator of art, each judge of truth and beauty, stands before the scales and weighs according to his own point of view. A food critic allergic to shellfish or tomato sauce can hardly be expected to offer culinary opinions on lobster newberg or veal parmigiana. A survivor of the Nazi holocaust ought not be expected to review objectively the books of Albert Speer or a concert of Richard Wagner's music. But just as our tastes and opinions are shaped in part by our biological systems and our personal histories, so too our aesthetics are determined by our "true intellectual and spiritual home," our base of operations, the platform on which we stand and from which we look at the world before us. From this platform we obtain the *Weltanschauung*, the world-and-life view which frames and focuses our understanding of the cosmos and all its complexities. If I am a nihilist, I see life and art as phantoms of meaninglessness, their reality to be scorned, and all belief in their permanence to be destroyed; therefore, my art and my critique of art will support the fundamental position I hold, that all is nothing. If I am a hedonist, I see life and art as a vast playground intended for my pleasure-making; my art and my critique of art will conform accordingly to my world-and-life view.

Frank Gaebelein chose as his place to stand the Word of God. Its revealed truth undergirded his life and formed his patterns of thought and expression. He was not too sophisticated to believe that

> The fear of the Lord is the beginning of wisdom;
> all who follow his precepts have good understanding.

In fairness, therefore, to any reader familiar with the formal philosophers of aesthetics, from Plato to Monroe Beardsley and John W. Dixon, Jr., a caution not to expect to find in

Gaebelein's essays the language and systems of philosophy. While his eclectic mind borrows from many, his spirit is sustained by one source. From that source Gaebelein derives his wisdom, his good understanding.

From the same pages of Scripture, Gaebelein also took his conviction that Christianity is not a religion only for the privileged, the healthy, the elite, the comfortable upper reaches of society. If literature, art, and music meant anything at all to Gaebelein, they meant that, as gifts from God, the arts are to be shared; so too with all the other means of grace from God's bounty. Christian faith must be expressed in acts of love and mercy, not withheld from those most in need.

A preaching mission throughout India and Pakistan opened Gaebelein's eyes to such appalling conditions as he had never before imagined; thereafter, he was earnest in giving his support to agencies such as World Vision and Bread for the World. So too in this country: When the racial disturbances in Selma, Alabama, were at their height, Gaebelein himself went to report for *Christianity Today*. As the civil rights advocates began their march toward national recognition of the justness of their cause, Frank Gaebelein stepped from the curbside and joined that march. A decade later, he was among the original conveners of the Chicago Call for a statement of social concern and action by evangelical Christians. It is fitting that his final major address should have been a speech delivered at the annual meeting of the Evangelical Theological Society, "Evangelicals and Social Concern." For Frank Gaebelein knew and believed that God's greatest work of art was man and woman made in God's own image, living out that image in love of God and love of neighbor. How, then, could anyone speak and write about truth and beauty in the arts unless one's heart was also warm to the needs of suffering humanity? As his daughter Dorothy Gaebelein Hampton observes, "During the last twenty years of his life, my father's major interest was to help evangelical Christians become more aware of our responsibilities to care for the needs of others."

This book stands as a posthumous testimony to the witness and influence of Frank E. Gaebelein's thinking. It is not, however, the book that he intended to write. That book may have had its genesis as early as 1950, when he was preparing his first truly significant work, *Christian Education in a Democracy*. Published by Oxford University Press in 1951, the report of the National Association of Evangelicals' Committee on the Philosophy and Practice of Christian Education counterbalanced an earlier secular treatise, *General Education in a Free Society*, the so-called Harvard Report. *Christian Education in a Democracy* argued for the revival of a distinctly Christian approach to learning and teaching, with a high priority placed upon the liberal and fine arts. The following year, in his seminary lectures at Dallas, Gaebelein attempted to spell out how such a revival might be achieved. From these lectures came *The Pattern of God's Truth: Problems of Integration in Christian Education*, also published by Oxford University Press, in 1954. Not by his own choice but by the demand of others, Frank Gaebelein's name became synonymous with the highest ideals in the philosophy of Christian education.

Years before, a young Long Island journalist had visited Gaebelein's office at Stony Brook to inquire about Christian service. "Get a solid education," the headmaster had advised. The young newspaperman took that advice and in remarkable ways, under God, has blended scholarship and journalism, theological acuity and powerful prose. His name is Carl F. H. Henry. In 1956, Henry was summoned by the founders of *Christianity Today* to become its first editor. Among the first he named as consulting editors was Frank Gaebelein, who contributed frequent essays and columns to the evangelical magazine. When, in 1963, Gaebelein laid down his responsibilities at Stony Brook, Carl Henry welcomed him to *Christianity Today* as coeditor.

Now began a new period in Gaebelein's life. For forty-one years, he had been a part-time writer and editor, squeezing in what time he could spare from administrative duties. At *Christianity Today*, he often lamented the time spent in rewriting other

people's prose—Gaebelein seldom found a theologian who
could write clearly and plainly!—but he nonetheless found time
enough to produce a substantial number of editorials and essays
of his own. Some of these were collected for *A Varied Harvest*
(Eerdmans, 1967) and are reprinted in this volume. Others he
retained for a project growing ever more important in his imagination and dearer to his heart. He would write a book of essays
dealing with Christian aesthetics. On a sheet of yellow legal-
size paper he wrote in pencil,

Title: Whatsoever Things

and followed this with a dozen proposed chapter titles.

Such a book had been on his mind for several years. In a
letter to Clyde S. Kilby at Wheaton College, dated 13 December
1957, Gaebelein had said,

> By the way, a particular book that I strongly feel
> needs to be written is a volume dealing with the sub-
> ject of aesthetics from the Christian and Biblical
> point of view. Do you have any suggestion for a
> writer of such a book?

By 1 April 1966, just as he was preparing to conclude his stint at
Christianity Today, Gaebelein had decided to be that writer him-
self. On that date he wrote himself a two-page "Memorandum
on Aesthetics and Christianity" which, along with another pro-
totype of things to come, "The Attainment of Truth in Art,"
formed the basis for the series of lectures he was to give at
Houghton College, at Bethel College and Seminary, at Denver
Seminary, at Trinity Evangelical Divinity School, at Multnomah
School of the Bible, at Trinity Bible Church of Phoenix,
Arizona, and at his home church, Fourth Presbyterian,
Bethesda, Maryland.

The keynote for all these essays and lectures may be found
in an undated fragment, headed "The Relation of Truth to
Beauty."

Despite Keats' famous line, truth is not to be completely equated with beauty. While in the deepest
sense truth is beautiful, because God is absolutely
beautiful in his perfection, nevertheless the two—
truth and beauty—are not synonymous. The reason
is that, although beauty can communicate truth, it
can also communicate a lie. Ethically, beauty can be
deceptive and downright evil. (The serpent in Eden.
Lucifer, an angel of light.) There are various works
of art which are decadent and at the same time beautiful; there are those which are corrupt and seductively
appealing aesthetically. One does not have to go far
to find examples—Baudalaire's *Fleurs de Mal*,
Picasso's erotic drawings, many contemporary
movies, Jean Genet, a beautiful writer devoted to
evil, etc.

On the other hand, truth cannot be evil, because
for it to be so would be a contradiction in terms. For
truth to be a lie would be, of course, to deny its very
nature. Truth is of God and anything evil is therefore
completely incompatible with truth.

In the summer of 1980, Gaebelein entered into correspondence with the editors of Multnomah Press regarding his proposed book. He presented his prospectus with customary directness:

In what way will my book be different from other
treatments of Christianity and the Arts? I can put this
under three heads: (1) It will be one of the few books
of its kind written by a recognized practitioner of two
of the arts—music and writing. (2) It will differ from
most writing about Christianity and the Arts in its
specific biblical orientation. Most writers on Christianity and aesthetics deal with the subject either
philosophically (Schaeffer, Wolterstorff, and Seerveld) or theologically (Sayers, Nathan Scott, Lynch,

and other Anglican and Catholic writers). I admire much of their work and am indebted to it. But my book will be distinctive for its integration with the Bible itself, though it will necessarily deal with the theological and doctrinal aspects of its subject. (3) The book will do something that has rarely been attempted—viz., it will deal carefully and at length with the difficult subject of the relation of truth to the arts. This will be one of its unusual features.

A contract was signed in January 1981, two months after his wife's death. Weakened by both his loss and his own declining health, Gaebelein nonetheless attempted to pull together the scattered pieces of his project to form a cohesive book. At the same time, however, he was struggling to complete the editing, volume by volume, of the massive *Expositor's Bible Commentary* and finding once again frustration over how badly most theologians write the English language. To his own dismay—and much to our loss—Frank Gaebelein never finished his book on aesthetics.

The Stony Brook School dedicated its new academic building, Frank E. Gaebelein Hall, in October 1982. The Headmaster Emeritus himself was there, walking slowly up Chapman Parkway to the platform alongside his friend, Senator Mark 0. Hatfield, the day's principal speaker. Hundreds of well-wishers greeted the aged guest of honor on this, his last appearance at the school he loved. On 19 January 1983, following open-heart surgery at the Mayo Clinic in Rochester, Minnesota, Frank Ely Gaebelein, after almost eighty-four years, entered into the presence of his Lord.

PART 1

THE AESTHETIC PROBLEM

The Aesthetic Problem

*I*n recent years, evangelicalism has been coming of age intellectually. With the strengthening of academic standards in many of its schools, colleges, and seminaries, its tendency toward anti-intellectualism has declined. More evangelical educational institutions have been accredited by the great regional associations since 1950 than in the preceding half-century. An increasing number of scholarly books are being written. And one of the major developments in religious publishing during the past decade has been the willingness of leading secular publishers to bring out the work of evangelical thinkers.

But a parallel tendency toward what may be called "anti-aestheticism" remains. In Dorothy Sayers's introduction to *The Man Born to Be King*, an essay every Christian student of the arts should know, she speaks of "the snobbery of the banal." It is a telling phrase, and it applies to not a few evangelicals. They are the kind of people who look down upon good music as highbrow, who confuse worship with entertainment, who deplore serious drama as worldly yet are contentedly devoted to third-rate television shows, whose tastes in reading run to the piously sentimental, and who cannot distinguish a kind of religious

51

calendar art from honest art. For them better aesthetic standards are "egghead" and spiritually suspect.

The arts pose uncomfortable problems for many evangelicals. There are those who question the relevance of the arts to Christian life and witness in these days of world upheaval. "Why," they ask, "spend time in this tragic age talking about such things as aesthetics?" The answer is that art belongs to human life. Pervasive and influential, it is an essential element of man's environment. And when art is unworthy, man's spirit is debased. "The powerful impact of modern culture upon modern man . . . discloses," as W. Paul Jones of Princeton says in an important essay, "the overwhelming degree to which contemporary man is being formed by an 'art' not really worthy of the name"[1]

Art, though aesthetically autonomous, has deep spiritual and moral implications. Like the capacity for worship, the aesthetic sense is one of the characteristics that sets man apart from the animals. Evangelicals turn away from art as a side issue or frill at the peril of their own impoverishment and at the cost of ineffectiveness in their witness. For art, which is the expression of truth through beauty, cannot be brushed aside as a luxury. We who know God through his Son, who is altogether lovely, must be concerned that the art we look at, listen to, read, and use in the worship of the living God has integrity.

Our God is the God of truth. According to the Gospel of John, "whoever lives by the truth comes into the light." This great principle is just as valid aesthetically as in doctrine and in practical living. Art that distorts the truth is no more pleasing to God than any other kind of untruth. Surely it is not too much to say that the God of all truth looks for integrity in artistic expression as well as in theology.

Some evangelicals may not like art. Because of their cultural illiteracy, they may be ill at ease in the presence of worthy artistic expression. In their discomfort they may want to say to the aesthetic side of life, "Go away, I'm not interested. I don't want to be bothered by you." But it will not go away. Through millions of radios and television sets, through the printed page, through advertising, through the architecture and furnishings of public buildings, churches, and homes—in a thousand and one ways art is here, though often in unworthy forms, and no one can run away from it.

Moreover, Christians have an aesthetic problem not merely because of the ubiquity of the arts but because in one way or another much in the contemporary use of literature and the arts is debased and opposed to the truth and to the values to which Christians are obligated. Evangelicals had better be concerned about the aesthetic problem, if for no other reason than that a tide of cheap and perverse artistic expression is constantly eroding the shoreline of noble standards and godly living.

The situation is complicated by the multiplication of leisure hours in this automated age. How many now use their extra hours wisely? Gresham's law may well have an aesthetic counterpart in that bad art like bad money drives out the good.

As background for some answers to the problem, consider a very brief survey of the aesthetic situation among many evangelicals today with particular reference to music, the visual arts, and literature.

Music is an area in which "the snobbery of the banal" stands in strange contrast to the doctrinal discrimination of many conservative Christians. Not only does the mediocre drive out the good; there is also a certain intolerance of the excellent that refuses to see that great music can be a far more true expression of a biblical theology than piously sentimental music. Or it may be that certain kinds of music finding ready acceptance in some churches reflect a theology that, despite its high claim to orthodoxy, yet leaves much to be desired.

Religious music, however, is not the only music we hear. Much of nonreligious music—serious and not just popular in character—betrays the spiritual rootlessness and moral anarchy of the times, as in the strident and heartless works of some of the atonalists or the irrationalities of the avant-garde composers. Thus there is all the more reason for inculcating in God's people higher standards for this great art that speaks so directly to the emotions and to the spirit.

Look next at the visual arts. Here, as in music, there are great riches. Granted that much in modern painting is related to the spiritual alienation of the day (although not all abstractionism is unworthy), how slight is the acquaintance of many evangelicals with the masters, past and present. How many know the works of American masters like Stuart, Inness, Ryder, Winslow Homer, Cassatt, Marin, or Andrew Wyeth? And what of the priceless treasures of great Christian art through the ages? There is vastly more in religious painting than the ever-present head of Christ that seems almost to have become a Protestant icon.

As for literature, where are the first-rate Christian novels and poems? Evangelicals have made notable progress in scholarly writing, but their achievement in more imaginative forms of literature is mediocre. Christian editors know the paucity of verse by evangelical writers that even begins to qualify as poetry. And in the field of fiction, distinguished novels and short stories written by evangelicals today are almost nonexistent.

Perhaps one thing that holds evangelicals back is a certain cultural parochialism and fear of the world. The moral state of much contemporary literature is indeed appalling. Here the aesthetic problem is a spiritual one that cannot be divorced from the Christian conscience. But there are many books that evangelicals can and must read, including not only the great treasures of English, American, European, and other literature but also representative current writing.

At a Christian teachers' institute several years ago, I urged breadth of reading and ventured to give a brief list of some of the great works indispensable to a liberal education. In the discussion that followed, a young man asked, "What has Plato to say to a Christian?" The answer is that Plato and every other great writer and artist of the past or present has much to give a Christian not only because it is essential to know the main currents of human thought but also because genius comes only from God. The doctrine of common grace asserts that God distributes his gifts among all kinds of men—unbelievers as well as believers. But the gifts are God's and the glory is his. Amid the moral corruption of our day, some great and worthy books are being written. Christians need to know them.

Like much else, culture begins at home. Taste is formed by what we live with. The question might well be asked of evangelicals: "What does your home tell of your spiritual and intellectual and aesthetic interests?" Said Rudyard Kipling in that subtle story, entitled "They": "Men and women may sometimes, after great effort, achieve a creditable lie; but the house, which is their temple, cannot say anything save the truth of those who have lived in it."

But this brief survey, which might well be extended to other arts such as drama and architecture, while necessary as diagnosis, points clearly to the need for action. Let us consider, therefore, three proposals toward evangelical answers to the aesthetic problem: (1) the formulation of a Christian theory of aesthetics based first of all upon the insights of the Bible rather than upon extrabiblical sources; (2) the cultivation of good taste and the development of the critical faculty; and (3) the revision of educational programs to give a more adequate place to the arts.

The Formulation of a Christian Theory of Aesthetics

Consider first the study by evangelicals of the theory of aesthetics. One of the hopeful signs of the last twenty years has been the development of a Christian and biblical philosophy of education. If evangelical education is experiencing renewal, the reason is that evangelical educators have been seriously occupied in considering the theological and philosophical basis of Christian education and in defining its goals.

But so far very little study has been devoted to aesthetics. Indeed, it is difficult to bring to mind a single published book by a conservative evangelical that deals competently with the theology and philosophy of aesthetics. Only comparatively recently have any Protestants given serious thoughts to this field. W. Paul Jones, in the article previously referred to, says, "Despite a history of virtual indifference to art, Protestant thinkers within the past several decades have begun to explore in earnest the relation of religion to aesthetic matters." Evangelicals should be joining in this effort. It faces them with an exciting opportunity to explore new paths in applying biblical truths to their cultural milieu.

The bulk of the work being done in the field of Christian aesthetics represents Roman and Anglo-Catholic thought. Its roots go deep into sacramental theology, Thomism, Greek philosophy, and such great writers as Dante. But in large part it is extrabiblical. There is a radical difference between the thought-forms of the Bible and those of Western philosophy and humanistic culture. And while the Bible says little directly about the arts or aesthetics, its basic insights must provide not only the foundation for an authentic Christian aesthetic but also the corrective for artistic theory derived from other sources, however excellent these may be.

Moreover, what some liberal Protestant thinkers have been doing in the field of aesthetics also needs revision, as Jones clearly points out. For Paul Tillich and others like him, he says, art is important because it is chiefly the indicator or "barometer of the 'faith' or 'ultimate concern' of a generation or culture." But the difficulty, he goes on to show, is that such a view of the function of art fails to discriminate between first-rate, second-rate, third-rate art, the latter of which often reflects the present culture more truly than the first! Art belongs to the only creature made in the image of God, the only creature to whom is given in a limited but real extent the gift of creativity, even though the gift is marred in fallen human nature. Thus considered, it is much more than the faithful mirror of culture. It is far more importantly a way-shower, leading on under God to fuller visions of his truth.

If there is, as we have seen, tension between many evangelicals and the aesthetic aspect of life, the reason lies in a contented ignorance of much that is aesthetically worthy and a satisfaction with the mediocre because it is familiar. Yet theological roots in the eternal biblical verities which never change do not necessarily imply enslavement to aesthetic traditionalism.

An essential element of true aesthetic practice is, as Alfred North Whitehead has suggested, the adventure of new ideas and their development in new forms. Let us remember that the great artists of the past had in their day an element of newness and spontaneity, and the greater the art the more abiding the newness. In a time when the ugly and the formless have become a cult reflecting the confusion of the pagan world, the creative Christian spirit in art should be pointing the way forward and upward, but always with reference to the everlasting and ever-present truth of him who is "the same yesterday and today and forever."

The Development of Critical Discrimination

A second proposal is that evangelicals must, if they are really to wrestle with the aesthetic problem, take seriously their obligation to develop critical discrimination in the arts. Good models are absolutely essential for sound aesthetic judgment. Good taste is not expensive; it is just discriminating. And it can be developed. Its formation begins very early.

It matters everything what kind of pictures are looked at by children, what kind of music is heard, what kind of television programs are viewed. Art exists in its own right, not just as a vehicle for moralism. Yet it cannot but affect those who are exposed to it. For young people to live day by day with shoddy literature and vulgar entertainment may tear down what they have heard in church and learned in Sunday school. Evangelical churches have picnics and hikes, athletic games and parties for young people—wholesome means of fellowship indeed. Why not also Christian fellowship in group attendance at a symphony concert, or a violin or piano recital? And it is surely not beyond reason for Christians to visit art galleries together. "The way to appreciate beauty," said William Lyon Phelps of Yale, "is to keep looking at it, to appreciate music is to keep listening to it, to appreciate poetry is to keep reading it."

At the end of the first chapter of Romans, after his appalling catalogue of sins within the human heart and life, Paul states the ultimate condemnation of unregenerate man when he says that they "not only continue to do these very things but also approve of those who practice them." As people look together at what is unworthy and debased aesthetically, they are together debased. But the converse is true. The shared experience of great music or drama, living with good pictures (even in reproductions)—these are group experiences in nobility and, let it be added, in reality. Not all music is joyous, nor does all drama have a happy ending. Yet, as Aristotle shows in his *Poetics*, tragedy purges the emotions through pity and fear. And at the pinnacle of involvement through experience in the company of others is the reverent worship of the living God, not for the sake of what we get out of it, but because God is God and because worship must be given him.

The time is overdue for evangelicals to outgrow their careless unconcern for aesthetic values and to develop critical standards that will enable them to distinguish good from bad in the art that surrounds them.

The Revision of Educational Programs

The third proposal, obvious but nonetheless important, concerns the more adequate place that the arts ought to have in Christian education. In too many evangelical schools and colleges the arts are little more than poor relatives of the curriculum. Yet in actuality they are not marginal, peripheral subjects; they are close to the heart of Christian life and witness. At present evangelical education is strongest aesthetically in music, although even here it yet has far to go. When it comes to the visual arts such as painting and architecture, and to the other performing arts, including drama, much of evangelical education is like a fallow field that needs both planting and cultivating. Christian schools and colleges must practice the unity of truth they preach by giving the arts a greater place in the curriculum.

The compelling motive for Christian action in the field of aesthetics lies in the nature of God. Christians are obligated to excellence because God himself is supremely excellent. In the Hall of Fame at New York University, these words are inscribed in the place given Jonathan Edwards, the greatest of American Christian philosophers: "God is the head of the universal system of existence from whom all is perfectly derived and on whom all is most absolutely dependent, whose Being and Beauty is the sum and comprehension of all existence and excellence." It is because of who and what God is, it is because of the beauty and truth manifest in his Son, it is because of the perfection of his redeeming work, that evangelicals can never be content with the mediocre in aesthetics. Here, as in all else, the call is to the unremitting pursuit of excellence to the glory of the God of all truth.

"The Aesthetic Problem," Notes

1. W. Paul Jones, "Art as the Creator of Lived Meaning," *The Journal of Bible and Religion*, July 1963.

The Aesthetic Imperative

*T*he subject of this essay, to put it informally and bluntly, is "The Arts Are a Must." Phrased in this way, it sounds drastic. "After all," someone may say, "isn't it rather radical to declare that the arts are a must? We think they are a good thing. They have a place in education and in life. When it comes to the main business of Christian life and service, they're a pleasant and helpful accessory. But to say that they are actually an imperative, and a must—well, isn't that going too far?"

No, I don't think it is—not if we stop and look at the arts in relation to the living God, who is the Giver of all good gifts, and not if we face up to the responsibility of offering him the best we are capable of.

Nevertheless our subject, with all its urgency, must be viewed in the setting of other biblical imperatives. Central to all we do is the obligation to glorify God and enjoy him forever. This, as the Westminster catechism says, is our "chief end." In fulfilling this end, obedience to the Lord according to his calling of us and through the personal gifts he gives us is essential.

Again, no responsible Christian will deny that the commandment of our Lord to make his gospel known—in other words, the witnessing imperative—is mandatory for every Christian. But this imperative has many facets, for we witness not only by words but also by what we are and do—yes, and by how we use the capabilities and talents we have.

Our Lord's Great Commission includes the obligation to teach everything he has commanded us. He said some very plain things about stewardship and our responsibility for using to the utmost of our ability what God has committed to us.

The Bible sets forth an exalted standard for the worship of God and it gives the arts a real place in this worship. When it comes to the common daily use of God's gifts, the arts among them, the Bible is neither repressive nor obscurantist. It teaches us that in a very special sense we, as well as the world we live in, are God's creation, that all we have, including our ability to make and respond to art, comes through God's grace, which he exercises according to his sovereign will. Thus we do God no honor, if we look down upon or stultify the artistic faculties or the worthy products of these faculties as merely worldly or un-spiritual.

For Christianity is an incarnational religion. It is God's truth embodied in real life; it is not a system of other-worldly, insubstantial ideals, like Platonism or Gnosticism, a tendency which has crept into some pietistic and evangelical circles where the arts have been considered as merely worldly or only secular. Surely it ill becomes us Christians whose Savior entered this real world in his true humanity, a Savior who died on a very nonideal and agonizingly real cross for our terribly real sins; who was buried in a tomb of hard, real stone; and who rose in a real body—it ill becomes us to look down on the arts as somehow lacking in spiritual significance.

They can reflect and shed light upon the deep realities of human life, such as human lostness and sin, the ambiguities and tensions we are faced with, and also and positively the glorious realities of redemption and of wholeness of being in Christ. They can do this not only symbolically but also with a wonderful directness of vision—as in the visual arts and in the literary arts—or indirectly as in the wordless eloquence of music. But we have to take time to see and listen to what they say about God and the world around us—and about ourselves also.

In one of the "Peanuts" cartoons, Lucy said to Charlie Brown, "The whole trouble with you is that you don't want to listen to what the whole trouble with you is." Granted that we who are Christians have found our identity in Christ, yet out of love and concern for others and readiness to face our own problems—and we Christians have them—we must be willing to listen to what the arts, especially in their contemporary forms, are saying regarding the trouble with people today.

Everything true belongs to God. There is truth in the arts as there is truth in science, history, or mathematics.

Let's look at the "aesthetic imperative" now in the clear light of Scripture. Come with me to the Old Testament where, in the book of Exodus (chapters 31 and 35), there's a significant mention of a great artist, Bezalel. God had given Moses the pattern for making a very beautiful structure, the tabernacle, with its wealth of redemptive symbolism wrought in the materials of wood, fabrics, colored dyes, and metals. Then—and I say it reverently—the Lord himself commissioned an artist to turn it into a reality. Listen to the record:

> Then the Lord said to Moses, "See, I have chosen Bezalel son of Uri, the son of Hur, of the tribe of Judah, and I have filled him with the Spirit of God, with skill, ability and knowledge in all kinds of crafts—to make artistic designs for work in gold, silver and bronze, to cut and set stones, to work in wood, and to engage in all kinds of craftsmanship. Moreover, I have appointed Oholiab son of Ahisamach, of the tribe of Dan, to help him. Also I have given skill to all the craftsmen to make everything I have commanded you" (Exodus 31:1-6).

Observe that the Lord not only gave Bezalel artistic talent; he also gave him an assistant named Oholiab, similarly gifted.

Not only so, but the Lord commissioned both men to teach others. For the parallel account in Exodus 35 adds this:

> "And he [the Lord] has given both [Bezalel] and Oholiab . . . the ability to teach others."

These two artists were to teach others their craft. Thus we have the first school of the arts among God's people! But let's look further at what the record tells us regarding Bezalel. Twice we are told that the Lord chose Bezalel by name—an unusual statement, somewhat parallel to the Lord's naming of Abraham and Jacob. Surely it points to the fact that artistic talent is an election of God.

Do you know what the name Bezalel means? It means "in the shadow [or protection] of God." So here was a man who may well stand as the prototype, the example, of the godly artist and craftsman in any field—a man, in this instance, to whom the Lord gave ability for a lofty purpose—to make his truth known through the construction of the tabernacle. And, as his name implies, Bezalel lived and worked under the Lord's own shadow or patronage. Think of it! The Lord himself the divine patron of the arts! How dare we, his creatures, ever look down on and neglect what he honored?

Observe also the kind of artist Bezalel was. He was a craftsman. He worked with his hands. And where would the arts be without these hands of ours—hands to draw and paint and fashion things—hands that gesture, and make music, and write—that stand as executors of the eyes that see and ears that hear and the minds and emotions that conceive and feel the art they express? Again, we think of the incarnational aspect of art, even as—and the reference must be made with reverence—even as our Lord Jesus made things with his hands. And who would question that, as a carpenter and craftsman, he made them beautifully?

But let us move forward to Christ's own teaching. Think of the parable in Matthew 25, the passage in Scripture that has given us the word *talent* as the synonym for ability. While the primary application of the parable is doubtless to spiritual gifts or capacities, it certainly may also be applied to the artistic gifts God endows us with and holds us accountable for. In this parable are the significant words, "each according to his ability." But you know the story—praise for those who developed their talents; condemnation for the one who buried his.

I have known people with very good musical talent who have said, "Now that I have become a Christian, I will dedicate my talent to the Lord." So far one can only rejoice, because every Christian with any kind of artistic gift should do this. But what do we say when some declare, "Therefore, I will play or sing only hymns or other religious music," and in doing this are often quite uncritical of the quality of the music they confine themselves to? This may not be the dedication but the burial of God-given talent. If so, it comes from the fallacy of considering sacred only that which is thus labeled, regardless of its artistic integrity, and considering as secular what is not labeled as sacred. But inferior art doesn't become true and good art because it is baptized by religious usage. An inept piece of religious verse doesn't become a genuine Christian poem because it says some things that are doctrinally correct. Nor are the sentimental pictures of our Lord that are so ubiquitous that I have come to think of them as evangelical icons—nor are these good art despite the good intentions behind them.

Why should we be concerned with excellence in the arts? Simply because of God's surpassing excellence in creation and beauty as in all else. As Jonathan Edwards said: "God is the head of the universal system of existence from whom all is perfectly derived and on whom all is most absolutely dependent, whose Being and Beauty is the sum and comprehension of all existence and excellence." Such a God demands our best in the fullest use of our talents and our grateful use of their products to the glory of God.

The arts may not specifically give the altar call, but the Bible makes it very plain that God has given them a true function in his service. They can bring glory to God whenever and wherever they are truly and faithfully practiced and thoughtfully enjoyed. For there's a sense in which all art is a celebration of him.

What now of art that is not directly linked with the worship of God? What about so-called secular art—art as inspiration and enlightenment, or as just plain recreation and enjoyment? Yes, and what about good and great art made by unworthy and unbelieving men? Does the aesthetic imperative apply here? I believe it does, provided that we see clearly that art may be subject to the most terrible misuse by good as well as bad persons. In the chapter in Exodus immediately following the one in which the Lord first called Bezalel under his patronage, we are told that Aaron took a tool and fashioned a golden calf. There are depths of meaning here about the misuse of the arts. They may be debased and perverted to wrong use. Like all human endeavor—business, science, education, government—the arts may be corrupted and turned into idols. Just as civil religion may become a substitute for the true worship of God, so cultural idolatry may take the place of our practicing and using the arts for the glory of God. But if this happens, the fault is never that of the divine Giver of our talents but always that of us to whom the arts are entrusted as a stewardship.

Now at this point we must face a vital question. What about the undeniable fact that some very great art in all fields is the work of non-Christians? Surely the answer can't be that we should refuse to have anything to do with it. To measure art and our use and enjoyment of it by the personal worthiness of those who make it or have made it would land us straight in a cultural ghetto. Even more, it would be dishonoring to God. He gives genius and talent to whom he wills. Theologians relate this to God's common grace, and common grace has its very important bearing on the Christian use of the arts. To put it bluntly, for a Christian to say, "I will not have anything to do with the great and worthy works of artists whose lives were not good," is to fall into the impiety of questioning the wisdom of God in bestowing the gifts of his grace where he wills. Let us then, for example, use and enjoy the so-called secular compositions of Bach, who was a Christian, but let us not turn our backs on the music of Wagner, who was neither a Christian nor a good man, or that of a Shostakovich, who was a communist. Likewise with the other arts. There must be an honest openness and catholicity in our use of them. The criterion must be their quality, not the kind of people the artists were or are.

A moment ago, I used the words *recreation* and *enjoyment*. This brings us to the everyday, contemporary aspect of the aesthetic imperative—not just for the professional or the gifted amateur, or the art or music major in college, but for all of us. In our time of radical change, the quiet revolution is the one that has taken place in respect to leisure. As free time has increased, the arts are demanding our attention as never before. In a real sense and whether we like it or not, we live in a context of the arts—and that not of the best. Through millions of radios and television sets, the paperback explosion, the electronic recording and amplification, through advertising, through the insistent, subtle persuasion of taped music in shopping centers, on airplanes, in dental offices—the arts are conditioning us as never before. So we are confronted with the necessity of discriminating lest we be smothered by the second rate and vulgar.

We Christians have an obligation not to submit passively to the cultural environment that surrounds us but to develop standards for judging it. The stewardship of leisure is a proper field for pastoral concern. The quality of our minds and thought is being determined largely by what we do with our free time. We can't escape the arts; they won't let us alone. And if I have spoken of discrimination and standards, I have not meant to imply that we should shut ourselves away from what is new and unfamiliar in the arts. We can't develop aesthetic standards and discrimination unless we are willing to be open-minded toward what is new and unfamiliar, even when we don't at first understand it.

Listen to the apostle Paul: "Finally, brothers, whatever is true, whatever is noble . . ." You know how eloquently his words flow as he goes on to speak of "whatever is right—pure—lovely—admirable . . ." And then he concludes with the imperative, "think about such things"; or as the Jerusalem Bible translates it, "Fill your minds with these things." Six categories of things to fill our minds with and nourish them on! And the first one, the things that are true, may well be the one that governs all the others.

Toward a Biblical View of the Arts

*O*ne of the fundamental musical forms is the Theme and Variations, in which a musical idea may be developed in all kinds of ways and in which new and related material may be introduced. Now in a sense the method I'm following in these essays is like that. In the previous essay we had, as it were, the basic theme—"the aesthetic imperative"—and we saw it in the light of some of the biblical background in Exodus and elsewhere.

In this essay I want to go right on with a development of other biblical material that underlies a Christian view of the arts. To take the Bible seriously, to submit ourselves to its authority as the infallible rule of our faith and life is not, as some seem to think, a hindrance to the practice and use of the arts. No, it's a tremendous asset, because the single greatest influence on the arts as we know them in our cultural heritage has come through Scripture; because in Scripture we have the great truths about man and God and the unending conflict and tension between good and evil that are at the well-springs of art; because Scripture gives the arts their greatest themes and highest motivation.

"That's quite a statement," someone says. "What about the fact that there have been times when Christians and the Christian church have been vehemently opposed to the arts? And what about the cultural illiteracy and suspicion of the arts that still survive among Christians today?"

Well, it's true that the church (and I'm using the term broadly) has been ambivalent toward the arts. There are those in it who still reflect the mood of the famous question asked by the Latin church father Tertullian seventeen hundred years ago, "What indeed has Athens to do with Jerusalem?" But there's another side of the coin. History shows that there have been times when the church and Christians have been influential supporters and encouragers of the arts. In fact, I'm optimistic enough to think that the period in which we are living may be on the way to becoming one of those times.

It's not the church, however, that we're thinking of now but the Bible. And here we find no ambivalence to the arts in themselves. Instead we find deep implications regarding them, for the Bible speaks to us about who we are and about our aesthetic responsibility under God. Moreover, we must never overlook the fact, so often forgotten by Christians, that God's inspired Word is itself a supremely great piece of art.

"What is man that you are mindful of him. . . ?" The answer to this question from the 8th Psalm takes us back to the opening pages of the Bible. It's a question we have to face if we are to think at all biblically and Christianly regarding our relation to the arts and indeed to the whole of culture.

So let's go to the passage in Genesis 1 that gives us the answer to this basic question about who we are.

> Then [i.e., after God's creation of the heavens and the earth and the whole procession of life culminating in the higher animals] God said, "Let us make man in our image, in our likeness, and let them rule over the fish of the sea and the birds of the air, over the livestock, over all the earth, and over all the creatures that move along the ground."

So God created man in his own image, in the image of God he created him; male and female he created them.

God blessed them and said to them, "Be fruitful and increase in number; fill the earth and subdue it. Rule over the fish of the sea and the birds of the air and over every living creature that moves on the ground."

Then God said, "I give you every seed-bearing plant on the face of the whole earth and every tree that has fruit with seed in it. They will be yours for food. . . ." And it was so (Genesis 1:26-29).

There in its own right, and also as it relates to its context in Genesis 2 and 3, is the basic passage in the Bible relating to a theology of the arts. It gives us the fundamental insight into who we are as human beings. It has long been called the cultural mandate, and rightly so. As Eric Sauer said, "These words declare our human vocation to rule and call us to a progressive growth in culture." Embedded in them is the fact that culture, of which the arts are such an integral part, is both God's gift to us and our duty—yes, our duty.

But this mandate is not, as some have wrongly supposed, to be blamed for the long abuse of the environment. It's a mandate for the responsible use of nature, as is clear from the complementary passage in Genesis 2:15, where the Lord God commanded man to cultivate and take care of the garden, which is the archetypical symbol of our environment. A while ago there was a cartoon in the *New Yorker* magazine that showed a portly, well-dressed man standing with his wife looking at a lovely vista of fields and trees. The caption was: "God's country? Well, I suppose it is, but I own it." But, of course, we don't own the earth; we're just stewards of it.

The earth is the Lord's, and everything in it, the world, and all who live in it.

In a sense we see in nature what some have called "the aesthetics of the infinite." It is not the mandate but the misuse of it that's responsible for environmental degradation.

But looking again at Genesis 1:26-29, we see that the cultural mandate doesn't stand alone but goes back to who we are and how God made us. Positively the greatest thing ever said of humanity is that God made us in his image. Consider how explicitly Genesis says it. First, the assertion of the divine intention—"God said, 'Let us make man in our image, in our likeness.'" Then the fulfillment of that intention with the double emphasis on "in the image of God he created him; male and female he created them."

"But," you may be saying, "what has all that to do with Christianity and the arts?" It has everything to do with it. Five times in Genesis 1, it is said that God "made"; five times that he "created." The Bible doesn't begin with a definition of who God is but with what he does. It begins with the God who acts. And conjointly with the statements about his action, five times the record tells us that what God did was "good" and a sixth time that everything he had done during the preceding creative days was "very good." Yes, the basic thing, as Dorothy Sayers shows in her book *The Mind of the Maker* (a study to which I'm much indebted), the basic thing Genesis 1 says about God is that he "makes." This is something that we have in common with him, for we too in our "creaturely" derivative way are makers.

So the image of God in us has its "creative" or "making" aspect. Obviously this image, which is one of the most profound subjects in theology, is much more than that. Yet this making or creative aspect of the image is a true part of it. For God is the Great Maker, the unique Creator. And all other creative activity derives from him. Here a caution is needed. When we use the words *create* or *creative* of art or any other human endeavor, we must realize that we are using them in an accommodated sense. Actually God is the only true Creator.

So we may agree with Keith Miller when he says, "In a real sense I believe God is presented in the Christian revelation as more of a living and creative artist than as a philosopher or theologian." It is in this authentic creative aspect of God, then, that the arts find their deepest sanction. When I was coeditor of *Christianity Today* a letter came in about an article I had written regarding Christian involvement in the arts. The writer called it "cutting paper dolls" in view of the serious business of the church. But this tendency among some Christians to belittle the arts as mere frills—optional, take-it-or-leave-it appendages to the main business of life—belittles and does dishonor to the Maker of all things who saw fit to create us in his own image.

Our capacity to make and enjoy art—to look at it and find it "good"—is a condition of our very humanity. As G. K. Chesterton said, "Art is the signature of man." No animals practice art any more than they worship. Subhuman creatures may make beautiful things, but only by instinct. The things they make— such as coral or honeycombs, spider webs or multicolored shells—are not their own conscious deliberate creation but an expression of God's thought. Only man consciously seeks over and over, and in some manner succeeds, in making art in varying forms and ways. Have you ever thought how far back man's aesthetic capability goes? Think of some of the prehistoric artifacts such as the Folsom points or arrowheads, perfect in their functional beauty. Or consider some of the cave paintings of the old stone age, made tens of thousands of years ago with a mastery that amazes us today. Why, before man ever had the alphabet he made art! As Francis Schaeffer has said, "Made in God's image, man was made to be great, he was made to be beautiful, and he was made to be creative in life and art. . . ."

But turn back to the repeated statement in Genesis 1 that God saw that his creative work was good and finally that it was very good. Surely here the word *good* has broad connotations of beauty.

Some contemporary artists and critics are inclined to downgrade the place of beauty in art. The cult of the ugly has its disciples. But Scripture links beauty to God and approves the beautiful. Moreover, by very definition aesthetics is the philosophy of beauty. The arts can't possibly be divorced from beauty. The problem is that there are those, some Christians among them, whose idea of beauty is just too small. It is not big enough to include the free use of dissonance and atonality in music, or to go beyond what is merely pretty or decorative in painting, traditional in architecture, or blandly nice in poetry and literature. Beauty wears various faces. And when it is authentic, it must, as Hans Rookmaker says, always be related to meaning and sense. And so, of course, it must be related to truth.

Like the Bible itself, beauty can be strong and astringent; it has disturbing and shocking aspects, as in tragedy or in painting, that reflect the protest and disintegration within our culture. It has its dark as well as comfortable moods.

Now essential as the basis of our human creative ability in the image of God is, this great fact does not stand alone. Genesis 1:26-29 with its cultural mandate must be viewed in the light of Genesis 3. Here is the point at which I have to criticize Dorothy Sayers, who in *The Mind of the Maker*, so brilliantly develops the analogy of the Trinity to our human creative processes. She and other Anglo-Catholic and Roman Catholic writers on aesthetics fail to give sufficient attention to the effects of the fall upon what man does in the arts. Something drastic, something humanly irretrievable, happened to the image of God in us when Adam and Eve rebelled against their Creator's command. Sin entered into the stream of humanity—sin with its inherent capability for all its protean manifestations down through the ages. None of us is an exception to Paul's great generalization: "All have sinned and fall short of the glory of God."

You and I know this through personal experience. We know that we can't save ourselves, that only God can restore us to himself and make us new beings through faith in his Son. Because of the fall, this world is, to use a phrase from one of Gerard Manley Hopkins's sonnets, "the bent world." Through sin a radical distortion has come into the world. It has affected every field of human endeavor. As Emil Brunner has suggested in his book *Revelation and Reason*, those areas of thought and activity that are closest to our humanness and our relation to God are most severely twisted by the bentness in us. And in the more objective fields like physics and chemistry they are less affected until in mathematics the distortion approaches zero. By such an estimate, the arts, which speak so subjectively and so very personally regarding who and what we are in relation to our Maker are very vulnerable to the distortion that sin has brought into the world. This means that Christian artists and all of us for whom the arts are an essential part of life and culture must constantly be keeping our eyes open to the marks of the fall in them and in us also. Aaron's misuse of art in taking a graving tool and making the golden calf symbolizes this.

Yes, this is "the bent world." The radical distortion that has come in through sin is a reality. The event Milton called "man's first disobedience and the fruit of the forbidden tree whose mortal taste brought death into the world" was ruinous. It did bring death. But this doesn't mean that man is essentially nothing, as some Christian people seem to believe. No, man is not a cipher. The Bible doctrine of the fall does not mean that we are totally worthless. The image of God in us has not been wiped out. By God's grace we can be redeemed. And by the exercise of his common grace humanity has been in the past and can still be today wonderfully creative to his glory.

So we come back to the matter of common grace. Have you ever wondered why some people who aren't Christians show more concern for others and have more of "the milk of human kindness" than many Christians? Or why some of the most beautiful things in all fields of art have been made by unbelievers?

Such questions can only be answered in terms of God's sovereignty in exercising his grace. It is only by his grace, his free and unmerited favor, that we are forgiven and redeemed through Christ. That's what theologians call special grace, and every Christian knows it firsthand. But God does not limit the exercise of his grace to the redeemed. That's a fact of history and of everyday life and it is backed by the Scriptures. By his common grace God restrains sin and prevents people from being as bad as they might be in their fallen state. By it order is maintained so that civilization is possible and culture may be promoted. We may well recognize in the founding of our nation the unmerited favor of God through his common grace. By common grace the benefits of the natural order are impartially given to all. As the Lord Jesus said in Matthew 5, "[God] causes his sun to rise on the evil and the good, and sends rain on the righteous and the unrighteous." And, according to the psalmist,

> The Lord is good to all;
> he has compassion on all he has made.

Likewise, and here we come to the essential bearing of this doctrine of common grace on our subject, God enables fallen men and women, whether saved or unsaved, to make positive contributions to the fulfillment of the cultural mandate through art. And he does all this through his Spirit working in the world and through human life.

Calvin has a powerful word regarding this:

> The human mind, fallen as it is, and corrupted from its integrity, is yet invested and adorned by God with excellent talents. If we believe that the Spirit of God is the only fountain of truth, we should neither reject nor despise the truth, wherever it shall appear unless we wish to insult the Spirit of God.

Did you ever think of genius as the great cultural phenomenon of God's sovereignty? Through those to whom he has given genius he graciously enriches human life. With a fine impartiality he gives genius and talent as he wills in all fields, of course, not just in the arts, and to all kinds of people. But always human responsibility accompanies the gifts of God's grace.

Now there is another biblical criterion for the arts that has hardly been mentioned so far, though it's been behind the scenes, as it were, in all we have been thinking about. An alternative title for this essay might well have been "Truth and the Arts." For the Christian concept of truth is implicit in our thinking regarding our practice and use of the arts. I touch on it now as a bridge to the essay following and to round out our discussion of some of the biblical roots of the arts.

God is ultimate reality. Therefore he is perfectly and in all fullness the Truth. God is the God of truth. So abundantly does Scripture show us this identity of God with truth that there's no need to cite special texts at this time. God is the God of truth. Christ his Son, who said, "I am the truth," is the Lord of truth, the incarnate Word of truth. The Spirit is, as Christ said, "the Spirit of truth," and the Bible is the written Word of truth.

Truth as presented in Scripture is not just an abstract, philosophical principle; it is as John said, truth to be done. Therefore we must recognize it and do it in the arts. All truth is God's truth. When I really began to take this axiom seriously back in the forties, it revolutionized my thinking about education and all of knowledge, the arts included. It unlocked for me the door to the integration of faith and learning. For if all truth is God's truth, then the separation that so many make between the sacred and the secular won't do. In God all truth has unity, though it may be of different orders or levels. We must see that the real distinction is between the true and the false, which means in the arts the distinction between what has integrity and so speaks truly and what is pretentious or sentimental, vulgar or shoddy, and thus is false.

In the scherzo of his Seventh Symphony, Beethoven quotes an old Austrian pilgrim hymn. In doing so, he uses an organ point, a tone sustained measure after measure as the fabric of the music goes on. The organ point is on A—the note to which the instruments of the orchestra are attuned. First, it sounds softly. Then it gets louder, till finally the brasses blazon it out in "a quivering flame of tone." It's one of the great places in music. So with the arts. Here, as in every aspect of life, truth is central, the thing with which everything else must be in accord.

INTEGRITY ←→ PRETENTIOUS/SENTIMENTAL/
TRUE ←   VULGAR/ SHODDY
          → FALSE

The Relation of Truth to the Arts

What is the function, the underlying purpose of art? What is it for? How many answers there are! Art exists to give pleasure, to edify, to represent or depict, to fulfill the artist's urge for making things, to tell us about life—so they go and they are helpful. For my part, I am impressed by what Denis de Rougemont says about this basic matter of the function of art. "As distinct from all other products of human action, the work of art is," he says, "an object of which the raison d'etre, necessary and sufficient, is to signify, organically, and by means of its own structure."[1] Hold in mind the idea that art has, as its reason for being, "to signify." Now de Rougemont goes on to tell us that, whatever its medium—sound, color, stone, wood, metal, movement, words—"the work of art has for its specific function the bribing of attention, the magnetizing of the sensibility, the fascinating of the meditation . . . and at the same time, it must orient existence towards something which transcends sounds and forms, or . . . words. . . . It is a calculated trap for meditation [and] a trap is made in order to capture something."[2] I think he is right.

79

Yet, some art is more demanding than other art; not all art is immediately captivating. Some is hard to know; the trap doesn't shut quickly. Have you ever thought of the patience that art can demand of us? It requires real patience to understand, even in part, some works of art, just as it required patience for the artist to make them. To take a personal example, recently I read for the first time Browning's very long poem, *The Ring and the Book*. It took patience to complete it, but I did it because this great poem does fulfill its function of signifying. It is indeed "a trap for meditation."

Here, then, is a broad criterion. Art that is true to its nature must in the long run command attention; it must be listened to, seen, heard, performed, as the case may be, and this voluntarily on our part who use it, and it *must* do this to signify. W. Somerset Maugham voiced a cardinal principle when he said in his preface to *The Razor's Edge*, "I want to be read." So the artist cannot but say: "I want to be played or sung, read or looked at; and I want to keep on being played, sung, read, or looked at."

If art does not hold our attention, it is frustrated and its maker also is frustrated, except for what its making may have meant to him. Indeed, it is a leading question whether some forms of contemporary art are not at the border line of futility and frustration, if not over it. But commanding attention in itself is not enough; signifying does not stand alone. The reason why great art keeps on compelling attention age after age is that it signifies something of truth. Nevertheless, to do this it must be looked at or heard. This is implicit in the very nature of things. It is a thoroughly biblical idea that creation is, as Emile Cailliet says, like a great signaling station telling us of God. So also art signifies in many ways—obliquely, metaphorically, sometimes in spite of itself, and its signifying is not lugged in, as in moralizing, but is inherent in its very form.

Thus we are led back to truth. "Art," said Francis W. Parker, "is the fundamental means of telling the truth," a statement we Christians may agree with, provided that we remember the inerrant telling of the truth in Scripture, which is indeed art at its highest, unique and inspired. By this standard, all human speaking of the truth is in a sense imperfect and incomplete; yet the artist, as best he knows how in his humble, creaturely way, must embrace this obligation to the truth. As Browning, the artist-poet, said at the close of *The Ring and the Book*:

> Why take the artistic way to prove so much?
> Because, it is the glory and good of Art,
> That Art remains the one way possible
> Of speaking truth, to mouths like mine at least.[3]

ASPECTS OF TRUTH

We all have a tendency to take great and familiar words like *truth* too much for granted. So let us look at truth and some of its basic aspects, for it's wrong to slide too quickly over the concept of truth. If we go to the dictionaries, we find truth equated with reality, fact, or actuality. Suppose someone suddenly tells you an astonishing piece of news such as: "My uncle has died and left me a bequest of twenty million dollars." You'd very likely exclaim delightedly, "Is that really true?" Now it's the adverb, the little word *really*, that swings like a compass needle to what we ordinarily mean by truth. Philosophers speak of this equating of truth with reality as the congruence or correspondence theory of truth, and it's one we all make use of. Similarly, there's the matter of the self-consistency of truth. We recognize that truth has integrity; it doesn't contradict itself. It may at times seem to be contradictory as in paradox, where truth is stated in a kind of upside-down way—"truth standing on its head to attract attention," as Chesterton has defined paradox. But essentially truth, having unity, can't go against itself.

Now in the Old Testament the words for truth denote firmness, fidelity, stability, reliability. The designation, "the God of truth," appears in Isaiah, Deuteronomy, and Psalms and describes him who is absolutely faithful and completely to be relied on.

In the New Testament, the word for truth suggests what is open, revealed for what it actually is, and therefore is neither

false nor devious. Here also it bears the connotation of faithfulness.

Arthur Holmes points out that the Bible contains three related aspects of truth: The moral one, the ontological one
(namely, that which is related to being), and the cognitive one
(that which is related to knowing). The first—the moral one—
concerns God's character and includes his integrity, his trustwor-
thiness, his faithfulness. And we, made in God's image, are obligated to reflect these in everything we do, the arts included. It
should be as disgraceful for a Christian deliberately to violate
integrity in art as to be dishonest in his business dealings.

The second aspect of truth in the Bible has to do with one's
really being what he purports to be. So the Lord Jesus spoke of
eternal life as knowing the only true God (John 17:3)—that is,
the God who is really the truth he purports to be. We on our
human level speak of a person as being a "true" Christian—or
talk about a "true" scholar or a "true" artist. So a work of art
must actually be what it purports to be.

The third biblical aspect of truth relates to knowing. The
Bible deals with truth as correspondence with fact and reality,
and reminds us that only God knows all things perfectly but, as
for us, we know only in part.

Here, then, is a frame of reference for our present inquiry.
Now suppose someone says, "But the arts are creative; they deal
with the realm of the imaginative and the intangible. Some of
them—the visual arts and music—don't really communicate in
words at all, but in ways quite apart from words." I think our
comment should run along these lines. Because the arts do indeed relate to the imaginative and the intangible and because
some of them speak to us apart from words doesn't mean that we
must exclude the arts from the tests of truth. Plain everyday
facts are essential, and when we speak about them in the arts,
we must do so truly as in a historical novel or play. But reality is
not confined to plain, everyday facts. Paul said in a context different from our present one, but in one of those great statements
bigger than its context, "For what is seen is temporary, but what
is unseen is eternal." And this shows us the wider dimensions of

reality. There is reality under God in the uses of the imagination and the intangibles, in the nonverbal in the arts—a genuine reality to which they must correspond.

Truth is such a spacious word, one that is so close to God for all truth is his truth, that we must be very careful how we speak about our relation to it, lest we fall into the sin of overweening pride the Greeks call *hybris*. There's one thing we must never say of truth—and this applies especially to those who deal with truth on the intellectual and creative level. We must never say of it, "I originated this or that truth. I made it up." We may say, "I discovered it," or, "I saw it," or "It became clear to me," but never, never, "I made it up all by myself," or, perish the thought, "I created it." How can we do this, when every bit of truth is God's in its perfect fullness? For whatever we do, truth is there all the time. Actually truth is in many cases a happening. I'm not speaking here of Scripture—the revealed written word of truth, though there's a sense in which truth here also happens to us when we believe what God has said. No, I'm speaking of truth as it comes to us when we exercise our capacity as makers in accord with the cultural mandate.

Long ago the truth of the hydrostatic principle happened to Archimedes, when the water in his bath slopped over and he ran out shouting "Eureka." The great French mathematician, Jules Henri Poincaré, told in a celebrated lecture he gave before the Society of Psychology in Paris how one of his fundamental mathematical insights came to him suddenly and unexpectedly while he was stepping on to an omnibus.

The history of science and of the arts is full of such happenings. In a letter to a friend, the composer Chopin said:

> Ideas keep creeping into my head. . . . I have too many themes . . . but when I write them down on paper . . . the thing is full of holes. . . . After a certain time a theme falls suddenly from heaven which will fit into one of these holes.

So musical truth happened to Chopin. Beethoven answered a question as to the source of his music in these words:

> You ask me where I get my ideas. That I cannot tell you with certainty. They come unsummoned, directly, indirectly—I could seize them with my hands—out in the open air, in the woods, while walking, in the silence of the nights, at dawn, excited by moods which are translated by the poet into words, by me into tones that sound and roar and storm about me till I have set them down in notes.

And there's a remarkable letter by Mozart, too long to quote here, that tells how truth constantly happened to him.

As for literature, we all know that the strangely beautiful poem *Kubla Khan* actually happened to Coleridge. But there are many examples. Go to the library and read John Masefield's preface to his *Collected Poems* and see how one of his longer poems came to him. And listen to this from an essay in the *Washington Post*, written upon the death of Arnold Toynbee, whose great work *A Study of History* brought him world fame.

> In 1921 returning from Istanbul on the Orient Express, Toynbee was visited by a sudden inspiration— somewhere in Bulgaria. . . . His ideas jelled and he scribbled on a piece of writing paper the 12 familiar headings . . . which defined the parts of *A Study of History*.

So we see that other things besides murder could happen on the Orient Express!

As for the performing arts, truth happens in them also. Here's an example told by the actress Helen Hayes in an address she gave in Washington. After quoting the producer Max Reinhardt's words: "The supreme goal of the theatre is truth," Miss Hayes described one of the many times she played Mary of Scotland:

> It happened one night in Cincinnati. It had been a dreary . . . rainy day . . . and I walked through the marrow-chilling rain to the theatre, longing as always to attain the unattainable. But when the curtain

rose . . . some ineffable spirit took over. I was Mary of Scotland . . . when Rizzio was murdered, my rage, a queen's rage, stunned the actors. My fury transcended everything. Actors who usually chatted with me backstage avoided me that night. (Even my dresser was silent.). . . In the last scene I returned, defeated by Elizabeth, to my old place in the recessed window of my cell and stared into the future. The curtain came down in deathly silence.

When I left the theatre, it seemed as if the whole audience was waiting in the alley. No one spoke to me. As I walked out the stage door, the crowd separated like the biblical Red Sea. Only when I reached the corner and turned into the street did they break into applause.

Now mark this. What happened to the actress that night happened to her audience also. That's one of the glories—and hazards too—of the arts.

Forgive me now, if for a moment, I expand our subject to include teaching, which is surely among the arts. In her autobiography Helen Keller tells how her infinitely patient teacher, Anne Sullivan, opened up the world from which in childhood her blindness, deafness, and lack of speech had isolated her. Anne Sullivan took her to a well-house and placed her hand under the cool stream gushing from the spout. Then into the other hand she kept spelling "water."

Suddenly I felt . . . a thrill of returning thought and the mystery of language was revealed to me. I knew that 'w-a-t-e-r' meant the wonderful cool something that was flowing over my hand. The living word awakened my soul, gave it light, hope, joy, set it free!

Haven't we who are teachers seen something like this happen when, after patient explanation, suddenly our pupil's face lights up and he says, "Oh, I see it now"? And haven't we who have been students experienced this kind of happening of truth?

Those of you who do art according to your dedicated ability, know that there are times when you do better than you know how. It's then that something of truth in art may be happening to you.

Now this matter of truth being a happening must never be leaned on as a crutch and never become a substitute for the hard discipline of craftsmanship, indeed the life-long discipline— which no one who works in the realm of ideas and the arts can do without. Truth happens to the prepared mind. I haven't the time to press the point. This mysterious and wonderful aspect of the creative process has been brilliantly discussed by the famous Catholic philosopher, Bernard Lonergan, in a book called *Insight*. Let me simply say that the happening of truth is related to commitment—which in the arts means long practice and dedication. There's a relationship here to Augustine's statement in the fifth century, "If you do not believe, you will not come to know." Or as Anselm of Canterbury put it in the eleventh century, "Believe that you may know." For the principle extends beyond religion. Believing in the sense of commitment can lead to knowing truth.

WHAT IS TRUTH IN ART?

So what is truth in art? What does a symphony or novel, a painting or a play, have to do with truth? Aesthetics has few more difficult questions than this. Yet the difficulty gives no excuse for not thinking about it, for the arts in one form or another pervade our environment and influence us all.

Marks of Truth

Let me now share with you what I take to be four marks of truth in the arts. They're descriptive and certainly not offered as final words on this subject. Truth is so big that we can't wrap it up in four neat packages or in four hundred! These marks seem to me like signs that, when we see them in various pieces of art, are saying: "Here is something that has truth."

There is, to begin with, the criterion of *durability*. Truth is of God. As such, it continues. Truth doesn't wear out. If a thing is true, it keeps on being true.

One of the great ancient works in aesthetics is the Greek treatise known as *Longinus on the Sublime*. Its author says this:

> That is really great which bears a repeated examination, and which is difficult or rather impossible to withstand, and the memory of which is strong and hard to efface. . . . For when men of different pursuits, lives, ambitions, ages, languages hold identical views on one and the same subject, then the verdict which results, so to speak, from a concert of discordant elements makes our faith in the object of admiration strong and unassailable.[4]

This is another way of stating the criterion of durability. Art that is deeply true does not succumb to time. It stands up to the passage of the centuries.

We must distinguish between durability in artistic works and the unique changelessness of God. "Jesus Christ is the same yesterday and today and forever"—that is eternally durable truth. So are the other great truths about God and man revealed in Scripture. These constitute Truth, as distinct from truth in art and other fields of human endeavor. In the latter, truth has durability but on the finite rather than eternal level.

But this, which is sometimes called the doctrine of universal consent, does not help us very much with what is newer in art. It is parochial to live only with the art and art forms of the past. Durability must not be pressed so far as to rule out contemporary art from any claim to lasting truth. Nor does the application of it always require many years: occasionally contemporary judgment quickly recognizes a masterpiece and is proved right by posterity. More commonly, however, great works do not come into their own till years after their creation. For example, Melville's *Moby-Dick*, now a secure masterpiece, was practically forgotten for decades. And Bach's *St. Matthew Passion* lay dormant for nearly a hundred years till Mendelssohn's revival of it revealed its towering greatness. I have a friend, the president of one of the most distinguished American secular publishing houses, who is devoted to music; he told me last year that he listens only to music of the baroque period and to no other kind. This is his privilege. But how much he misses! His is an extreme case, though I venture to say that among us Christians with our innate conservatism there is a good deal of suspicion of the new and contemporary in art—call it neophobia, if you please—and it is based more on ignorance than on considered judgment, as in the case of my publisher friend.

Think now of the opposite side of the coin. What T. S. Eliot said of readers today can be applied with reservations (largest in music) to the arts other than literature.

> There never was a time when the reading public was so large, or so helplessly exposed to the influences of its own time . . . there never was a time when those who read . . . read so many more books by living authors than . . . by dead authors . . . a time so completely parochial, so shut off from the past.[5]

We certainly have a right to be devoted to the new. But if we are exclusively devoted to the new in any art, then we had better not try to develop artistic judgment, because we need the past for a frame of reference. Otherwise we may have no sounder basis of values than the girl who, according to *Life* magazine, said, "When I hear a Beethoven symphony I don't feel anything. When I hear our kind of music [was it the Beatles?] I feel something way down deep like oatmeal."

2. Consider in the next place *unity* as a criterion of truth in art. Here again there is a deep theological reference, the analogy of the Trinity. And, in talking about art, we ought not to apologize for our theological references. As Dorothy Sayers says, "Right in truth is right art; and I can only affirm that at no point have I found artistic truth and theological truth at variance."[6]

The criterion of unity in art is very old and always relevant. Outside the Bible, it found classic expression long ago in Aristotle's *Poetics*. We may set it down as a principle that unity—unity of form and structure—is basic to truth in art. When a book or piece of music lacks unity, you don't have to know Aristotle to say, "It doesn't hang together."[7] The concept of order, which is related to that of unity, is implicit in the cultural mandate in Genesis. When God created man, he was placed in a garden and told to cultivate and keep it. Order is implicit in this idea of cultivating a garden. The creative process in man is not innately disorderly.

At its truest, art tends toward unity and order. The reason for this relates to the incarnational nature of art. As Goethe said, "The spirit tends to take to itself a body." In the arts, the concept or idea is given definite form; it is embodied in sound, color, or words; in wood or stone; in action or movement, as in drama or ballet. But embodiment requires unity and order; a body cannot function effectively in a state of disorganization.

Here we have to ask some questions about certain manifestations of contemporary art. Why not ask them of older art? Simply because the winnowing process of time has pretty much settled them. Today we are seeing in some important aspects of avant-garde art a centrifugal, schizophrenic tendency. And this fragmentary, disintegrating trend points to the lostness and rebellion of so many in this broken world. It is a barometer of the times (a point Paul Tillich stresses). Indeed, this is what its tendency to formless form, to put it paradoxically, signifies.

Is this, however, enough? Do we not have a right to expect art to be a way-shower rather than merely a barometer? Is it not a grave lack in some contemporary art that it "gives in" to its situation rather than controlling it and signifying beyond it? Does not this account for a certain loss of sublimity—a quality in short supply now—in contemporary art? Surely art that is ultimately true can do more than reflect what is. It can also have its prophetic function. The history of literature, music, and the other arts contains notable examples of genius that not only spoke to the present situation but went beyond it to break new trails for aesthetic advance. Beethoven knew rebellion and alienation through his deafness. Yet what makes him great is his mastery of these things and bringing them to a sublime resolution not only in peace but also in joy.

Now don't mistake the reference to Beethoven, who is an older model, as implying that only such forms as he used are valid. We should not rule out newer modes of musical or literary expression or abstract visual art. It is not a case of abstract versus representational, as in painting, for instance. Both may command attention and signify meaning; both may be true. It seems to me, however, that Jacques Maritain made a significant point when he said in his lectures at the National Gallery in Washington, entitled *Creative Intuition in Art and Poetry*, that among the drawbacks of certain abstract art is its tendency to deform the human face and figure, thus leaving art "in possession," as he put it, "of every means to express spirituality except the normal one." Not that he insists on literal representation, for he commends El Greco for changing the human figure "into something more human." (And doesn't Rouault belong here also?) What Maritain's criticism is directed at is rather what he calls "the school of degradation in art."[8] Is this trend linked to what Wylie Sypher in a recent study calls the "loss of self in modern literature and art," a kind of school of subtraction, so that one may end up with what Sypher terms "the zero degree of painting"?[9] If that happens, do we not have the nullification of the artist as maker of something that signifies? For what can nothing signify besides nothing?

Closely linked to the criterion of unity as pointing to truth in art is the principle, or criterion, of *integrity*. There is at this point a most lofty biblical reference in Paul's wonderful Christological passage in Colossians 1, where, speaking of our Lord Jesus Christ, he says: "He is before all things, and in him all things hold together."

Although unity and integrity have to do with basic form or structure, integrity is more comprehensive, having to do with the matter of wholeness. A novel may be structurally unified, yet fall short of integrity if the characters or dialogue are unconvincing. Integrity refers to the overall truthfulness of a work of art. When we say that a person has integrity, we mean his entire personality is morally sound. So it is with integrity in art.

In the arts, integrity demands that anything contrived merely for the sake of effect and not organically related to the purpose of the work must be ruled out. Regrettably, there is much in evangelical literature, music, and art that lacks integrity. Sentimental pictures of Christ are widely promoted, records dress up hymn tunes in commonplace variations, and fiction written by evangelicals rarely rises even to the level of competent literary craftsmanship. It is evident that many Christians have much to learn about integrity in their use of the arts.

What we need to do is to get back to our true Christian heritage. Reverently, let me say that we can learn much from our Lord's use of art. Think of the beautiful and completely memorable way he used words. "No one ever spoke the way this man does." Who can add a word to his parables of the Prodigal Son, or the Good Samaritan, or the Pharisee and the Publican? They are told without moralizing; their perfect expression is innate. Here is integrity in words at its highest. It is the kind of thing reflected on our imperfect human level in the great succession of authentic Christian writers and musicians and painters and architects and all the rest, a succession which has, thank God, some worthy representatives today.

Does the Christian artist have a plus factor here? I think he does; as a Christian, a redeemed man, indwelt by the Holy Spirit, who is the Spirit of truth and integrity, the Christian artist is in a position to tell with integrity the whole story, to go beyond where so much art stops, and to signify the full picture not only of man's alienation and lostness but of what God has done to redeem him. This added dimension has characterized the work of great Christian writers from Dante through Milton and Bunyan to Dostoevski, T. S. Eliot, Graham Greene, Francois Mauriac, and Flannery O'Connor. In a letter written about ten years after his conversion, C. S. Lewis said, "One of the minor rewards of conversion is to be able at last to see the real point of all the literature we were brought up to read with the point left out."

Integrity in art? It relates also to what we do with art and how we respond to it. To say we like what we really don't like, just because we think we ought to like it, is a kind of aesthetic pretense or lie unworthy of any Christian. Better simply say, "I'm puzzled by it; I don't get it; I don't understand it; but I'm willing to see, or read, or listen to it." In her novel, *The Song of the Lark*, which tells the story of a Colorado girl who becomes a great singer, Willa Cather says: "Artistic growth is, more than anything else, a refining sense of truthfulness."[10] That principle applies to our own day-by-day response to art as well as to the "creation" of art.

Look now at another criterion for truth in art—one that may be called the criterion of *inevitability*. Have you ever thought of what might be termed "the familiarity of the unfamiliar" in art that possesses real truth and integrity? For instance, you have heard for the first time a hitherto unfamiliar work by such a composer as Schubert, and the inevitability of certain phrases, their utter rightness, gives the impression, despite the piece's unfamiliarity to you, of something you already know. Or in painting you feel that a picture is completely right; it could not have been done any other way. Or in poetry, there is the sense that this is the inevitable expression of the poetic meaning. In such cases, we say, "This is right; this is how it ought to be."

John Keats in a letter to his publisher John Taylor, describing the kind of writing he hoped to achieve, seems to me to have pointed to this quality, when he said: "I think poetry should . . . strike the reader as a wording of his own highest thoughts and appear *almost a remembrance* [italics added]." And one of Haydn's contemporaries, the critic Ernst Ludwig Gerber, said of that great composer, "He possesses the great art of making his music oftentimes seem familiar." Perhaps this recognition may be delayed until we exercise the patience I have already spoken of, for true art does not always wear its heart on its sleeve; we may indeed have to wait until we know the work better and penetrate more deeply into it. But when we do this, we may well experience this quality of rightness or finality of expression, which is a sure mark of truth. It is, to lift the reference up to the biblical level, what J. B. Phillips calls "the ring of truth."

These four criteria—durability, unity, integrity, and inevitability—give us some insight into the nature of aesthetic truth. They are not the whole answer to the question "What is truth in art?" but they are components of it. And they are closely interrelated principles; each contains something of the others.

To these four marks of truth in art let us add two examples from art that is Christian. For here the criterion is the reflection of the reality of God himself.

The musically sensitive Christian who listens to a performance of Bach's B-Minor Mass experiences a supreme example of truth-telling in sound. Truth may be defined as correspondence with reality. The ultimate reality is God, and the Christian knows this reality in Jesus Christ, God manifest in human form. Anything in art that sheds light on this reality has truth at the highest level.

So consider a Christian hearing the B-Minor Mass. As he listens to the hushed sound of the "Crucifixus" with its mysterious downward progressions, he hears a tonal portrayal of the atonement that goes straight to the heart. Then, at the end of the "Crucifixus," there is the sudden outburst of joy in the "Resurrexit," as choir and orchestra acclaim the risen Lord Jesus Christ with a power few if any written commentaries ever attain. This presentation of the truth transcends barriers of language as it speaks to all Christian hearers. Aristotle spoke of art as mimesis or "imitation." Here is mimesis in the highest sense, as Bach puts into music the profound truths of Christ's passion and victory over death.

To turn to another field, consider Rembrandt's great portrayal of the supper at Emmaus. Here is truth in form and color. Unlike Salvador Dali, who painted a blond Christ on a cross suspended between heaven and earth, Rembrandt portrayed Christ with integrity. His pictures show us our Lord as he was—Jewish, a real human being here on earth. Yet when this great artist paints the supper at Emmaus, he gives us the very moment of truth when the disciples' eyes are opened and they see the risen Lord. The person they see is indeed human. We recognize him as the Christ, but Rembrandt shows us at the same time his glory. Here again we have truth in art, mimesis in its highest Christian sense.

But what about truth in lesser works of art and literature? Truth in art cannot be limited to the works of supreme genius. Wherever there is integrity, honest craftsmanship, and devoted cultivation of talent, there something of truth may break through. Literature has its minor classics and painting its primitives. Folk music can speak as authentically as a sonata. Honest craftsmanship, as in functionally beautiful furniture or pottery, enriches culture. And though these may not receive universal renown, they can attain a measure of truth.

BEAUTY AND TRUTH

No discussion of truth in art can be considered complete without some reference to the relation of beauty to truth. After contemplating an ancient vase, John Keats wrote his "Ode on a Grecian Urn." The final lines of the poem—" 'Beauty is truth, truth beauty,'—that is all/Ye know on earth, and all ye need to know"—seem to provide a definitive answer to the question.

Yet this identification of beauty with truth, so often taken for granted, needs scrutiny. Writers and other artists correctly reject the tendency to put moralizing into art. But do they have no moral responsibility whatever? Is art devoid of any ethical dimension?

The great biblical phrase "the beauty of holiness" answers with a qualified negative. Even if one were to grant autonomy to the beauty found in works of art, there still remains the artist himself. Like every human being, he stands under the ethical judgment of God. What he creates may be beautiful and aesthetically true. Yet it may tell a lie. The French writer Jean Genet writes beautiful prose, but his work is decadent. Picasso's erotic drawings are beautiful but corrupt. For the basic analogy, however, we need to go back to what Scripture says about Satan. There is a depth of meaning in Paul's statement that Satan himself is transformed into an angel of light. Beauty itself can become the vehicle for a lie.

To this possibility two kinds of beauty stand as exceptions—the chaste intellectual beauty encountered in such things as pure mathematics or scientific equations, and that beauty which Ernest Lee Tuveson has called "the aesthetics of the infinite." The latter is the beauty reflected in God's work in creation. The Scottish mountaineer W. H. Murray tells of seeing the Buachaille Etive More, the great peak in Glencoe, in brilliant winter moonlight:

> Let us speak of the unspeakable, for there is no speech so profitable. [Its] face was washed by intense light so searching that no shade was cast by ridge or buttress. All detail merged in the darkness of one arrowy wall, pale as shadowed milk, impregnably erect. At the remote apex, a white crest broke spume on the high seas of infinity. . . . To my unaccustomed eye the scene at first bore an appearance of unreality; yet the more I gazed, the more surely I knew that I saw not an illusion greater than is usual, but truth made manifest.

This was one of what Murray called those "fleeting glimpses of that beauty which all men who have known it have been compelled to call truth." Such beauty is incorruptible.

And what of the purely intellectual beauty of higher mathematics or scientific equations? The physicist Dirac maintained that the truth of an equation is evidenced by its beauty. So those who are trained to think in these realms recognize beauty in the balance and symmetry of conceptual thought and in the disciplined simplicity of symbolic logic. Just as a chess master speaks of a beautiful series of moves, so a mathematician sees beauty in numbers and symbols. On this level, beauty, while manifest through the mind of man, has a certain incorruptibility, even though it may be put to debased uses, just as the pristine beauty of nature may be despoiled by man.

But for most of the beauty man attains, Keats's identification of it with truth must always be qualified by the Christian
artist. Nor can he accept the finality of the poet's conclusion,
"that is all/Ye know on earth, and all ye need to know."

The Christian artist has to know more than this. He must
know his responsibility to God who gave him his talent, and he
must also know the misuses to which beauty is prone. Beauty is
not exempt from the consequences of the fall. Like money or
power, art may become an idol. Apostasy may assume angelic
forms. This is why the Christian artist stands so in need of humility; he must never depart from the priority of seeking to glorify
God in all he does.

To identify beauty with what is immediately pleasing or
captivating is to have a superficial view of beauty. The difference between a Rembrandt portrayal of Christ and one by
Sallman is the difference between depth and superficiality.

Moreover, to identify beauty exclusively with harmony
and orderliness does scant justice to the power and truth the arts
are capable of. Rouault's paintings of Christ are not convention-
ally beautiful, but they have the inner beauty of truth. Merely to
look at Grunewald's Isenheim altarpiece with its agonizing
crucifixion scene is to be confronted with the most terrible yet
true picture ever painted of Christ's suffering for the sin of the
world. Dissonance in music, stark realism in literature, and the
"ugly" in visual art all have an indispensable relation to beauty.
The concept of beauty in art must be large enough to include the
aesthetic astringencies. For Beauty wears different faces. There
is the unclouded serenity of Raphael in his *Alba Madonna* or the
seraphic slow movement of Mozart's last piano concerto. In
contrast, we have the thorny beauty of Browning in *The Ring
and the Book* or the rugged beauty of Bela Bartok's music.

To turn again to "the aesthetics of the infinite," the incorruptible beauty of God's handiwork in nature has its terrible as
well as its pleasing aspect. The bleak wastes of the Sahara are
beautiful in a different way from the smiling loveliness of a

Hawaiian landscape. Moreover, our apprehension of beauty changes as we develop our aesthetic faculties. Only comparatively recently have some of the greater aspects of natural beauty been appreciated. In the eighteenth century, majestic mountain scenery was often avoided rather than recognized as sublime evidence of God's creative power. Fashions in art and literature change. But elusive and difficult to define though it is, true beauty continues. Just as God has yet more light to shine forth from his Word, he has greater dimensions of beauty for us to comprehend in his creation and in man's making of art.

Therefore, besides being aware of the perils of the misuse of beauty, we must recognize that beauty has profound theological implications. Among the great theologians and Christian philosophers, no one saw this more clearly than Jonathan Edwards. He spoke of God as "the foundation and fountain of all being and all beauty . . . of whom, and through whom, and to whom is all being and all perfection; and whose being and beauty are, as it were, the sum and comprehension of all existence and excellence."

The relation of beauty to God, so profoundly developed by Edwards, means that we cannot downgrade the arts as side issues to the serious business of life and service, as some Christians do. When we make and enjoy the arts in faithful stewardship and integrity, they can reflect something of God's own beauty and glory. Through them we can celebrate and glorify the God "in whom we live, and move, and have our being."

"The Relation of Truth to the Arts," Notes

1. Denis de Rougemont, "Religion and the Mission of the Artist," in *The New Orpheus*, Nathan A. Scott, Jr., ed.

2. Ibid.

3. *The Ring and the Book*, at close of XII.

4. *Longinus on the Sublime*, trans. and ed. by W. Rhys Roberts, 57.

5. T. S. Eliot, "Religion and Literature," in *The New Orpheus*, Nathan A. Scott, Jr., ed.

6. Dorothy Sayers, *The Man Born to Be King*, Introduction, 3.

7. Cf. Dorothy Sayers, *The Mind of the Maker*, 11.

8. Jacques Maritain, "Beauty and Modern Painting," in *Creative Intuition in Art and Poetry*, 152-53.

9. Wylie Sypher, *Loss of Self in Modern Literature and Art*, 110.

10. Willa Cather, *The Song of the Lark*, 571.

Christian Responsibility in the Arts

*B*y the title of this essay I mean the responsibility of all of us to God and our neighbor for what we are doing about the aesthetic side of our lives. So we return to the basic matter of stewardship in the arts touched on in an earlier essay.

That you and I are stewards of God goes back to the cultural mandate in Genesis 1 in which God committed to humanity the responsibility of dominion over the created order of things. In the New Testament we find this principle of stewardship or responsibility focused on the gifts God gives us. Listen to the beautiful way it is stated in 1 Peter 4:10: "Each one should use whatever gift he has received to serve others, faithfully administering God's grace in its various forms." While the initial reference here is to spiritual gifts in the church, the wider application, as in the parable of the talents, is to whatever capabilities, artistic ones included, God has endowed us with. Always there goes with stewardship the inevitability of finally giving an account of what has been committed to us and of being judged on how we have used it. As Calvin Seerveld has said, "With all our getting of politics, economics, the sciences—we must get the arts too, lest when our Lord return for an accounting we shall have to dig up our one artistic . . . talent . . . and face his wrath."

Now first of all, we must consider an important matter so as not to slip into the fallacy of limiting Christian responsibility in the arts only to the specially gifted and forgetting the responsibility for aesthetic stewardship of the great majority of people who aren't artists. Because by no means all of us have special talents in the arts and because among those who are talented only a very, very few can honestly be said to have truly great talent, are the rest of us privileged to shrug off our personal responsibility in relation to the arts? Of course not! When it comes to the kind of things that make up our cultural environment and when it comes to our relationship with each other, the arts are the business of us all. Why? Because each of us has in one way or another an aesthetic faculty. Because we each have in some measure the capability of responding to artistic expression.

Have you ever heard someone say, "I just don't have any artistic sense at all"? Have you ever said it yourself? Well, don't say it, because it isn't true. Even though you were tone deaf or color blind, you would still have the capability of some response to the arts. That fact in itself is the one talent we all have in this field and we had better not bury it. Therefore, we're all accountable to the sovereign God, who made us as we are, for how we cope with the arts. And cope with them we must, because they're incessantly impinging on us all.

In one of his Christmas messages, Pope Paul VI saw the excesses of the mass media as among the world's leading problems and spoke of it in these words: "the deafening roar of a thousand voices which fill the atmosphere of modern life, the powerful loud speakers of the familiar means of social communication, or the suggestive lure of image and sound. . . ." No other generation in history has been more besieged by the arts in their big-money, people-manipulating use than ours. I don't have to spell out how this is happening through the movies, television, the printed page, radio, and in many other ways. Of course, not all of this is bad. Yet much of it is of a kind of ersatz, plastic nature that can dull our aesthetic sensibilities.

Therefore, Christian responsibility in the arts requires us to develop a tough critical-mindedness in relation to them. The fact is that most of us are entirely too passive regarding much that surrounds us in the arts today. In a series of lectures at the National Gallery in Washington, Jacques Barzun of Columbia University described our present-day tolerance of art as "amazing." "Art," he said, "is power; it can weaken or destroy the civilization that created it. It can enlarge or trivialize the imagination." He was right. And I would add to what he said that we must get away from the naive notion that because something passes for art it is therefore in itself of value. That's about as sensible as going to a department store and buying some daub of a picture for $39.95, because it's labeled as an original oil painting, or thinking that because we read something in a book it's true. Here is a passage from an essay by T. S. Eliot, whose prose is easier than his poetry.

> What is incumbent on all Christians is the duty of maintaining consciously certain standards and criteria of criticism over and above those applied by the rest of the world. We must remember that the greater part of our reading matter is written . . . by people who have no real belief in a supreme order.

What he says applies, of course, to the other arts also. You and I have no right to take the arts for granted. They are not neutral; they do something to us, and we need to be aware of what they are doing.

So I go back to T. S. Eliot because he said it so well:

> The author of a work of imagination is trying to affect us wholly, as human beings, whether he knows it or not; and we are affected by it . . . whether we intend to be or not. . . . Everything we eat has some other effect upon us than merely the pleasure of taste or mastication; it affects us during the process of assimilation, and I believe that exactly the same is true of anything we read. . . . Though we read literature

merely for pleasure [or I might add, see a movie, go to a play, hear music, or experience other forms of art] this never affects simply a sort of special sense; it affects us as entire human beings; it affects our moral and religious existence.

Now Eliot wasn't implying that art must moralize or be didactic. He was too great a poet for that. He was simply saying that art inescapably affects us. And he was right, despite the current and widespread claim that art of a debased or pornographic nature is somehow exempt from this principle. Remember that it is part of the nature of art to incarnate itself—that is, to embody itself. When we dismiss art as "just art" we forget its power. It may for some time only incarnate itself in words, color, patterns, or sound. "But," as Dorothy Sayers said, "the day comes when it incarnates itself in actions, and this is its day of judgment."

We simply have to have standards. Otherwise we can become enslaved to the culture around us. I'd as soon go to a medicine cabinet and gulp down at random anything in it than to pick up at a newsstand any book and read it. The mind and spirit need a balanced diet just as the body does. Too much cultural fat leads to intellectual and cultural flabbiness; too much heavy meat leads to intellectual and artistic indigestion; too many sweets lead to insipidness; and if we feed our minds and spirits on garbage—and there's plenty of it around these days—that's bound to lead to decay and putridity within us.

Now though the arts can be corrupt—and responsible Christian criticism must be aware of this—such criticism also recognizes what is good and true in them at various levels and gives God the glory.

But by what criteria do we judge the arts? Over and above the four criteria already mentioned as marks of truth, there always is the standard of excellence, the reaching for the best toward which responsible artists of all kinds strive according to their ability.

The distinguished British chamber music player Derek Simpson said of the Aeolian Quartet of which he is a member: "One of the wonderful things about our work is that every time we walk on the platform we're having a debut. It's not just another concert. It's to do with ethics of playing music because you're seeking for something you can never achieve: perfection." When we discriminate and criticize in the arts, we do so by the criterion of excellence and in reference to the goal of perfection. As Plato said, "Nothing imperfect is the measure of anything." Recall how, in the experience of Helen Hayes related in the preceding essay, she said that she walked through the rain to the theatre, "longing as always to attain the unattainable." That's the motivation of a true artist. Whatever the field, artists always want to do better. They can't settle for less than their best. If they did, they wouldn't be artists. The trouble with being satisfied with the mediocre either in doing art or enjoying it is that you can become addicted to it the way some people get addicted to soap operas.

"What you're talking about," someone objects, "is just elitism, high culture, so-called, and it's only for the few who can appreciate it. But the arts are democratic; they're for everybody." In reply, consider what Antal Dorati, the distinguished conductor, said in a recent interview. "Yes," he said, "the arts are part of an elite . . . but I do not say that [they] are not for everybody. . . . There are no closed doors to the elite. Everybody can belong."

Nothing short of the best will do as the standard for criticism. The God who gave us in his Son the one and only example of a perfect human life as our pattern of obedience has on the lesser level of the arts given us the high products of genius as examples of excellence. The arts have many varieties, and excellence in them takes different forms. So in the music we compose, the pictures we paint or designs we make, the stories we write, the parts we have in a play, the musical programs we give—we must desire to reach as far toward excellence as our best will take us. The greatest thing that can happen to us in the arts is to learn to do one thing really well. This applies to all of us, including those who are not practicing artists. To know how to read well is an art—and a basic one at that—and opens the door to the spacious palaces of literature, just as to know how to look and hear intelligently opens other doors in the other arts.

Doing something really well is what we call craftsmanship—the gift God gave Bezalel and Oholiab for making the tabernacle. One of the greatest and most Christian novelists of our times, the French Nobel Prize winner Francois Mauriac, said in his last book, *The Inner Presence*, written when he was eighty:

> My writings have benefitted from the fact that no matter how lazy I was, I always wrote the least article with care putting my whole soul into it. I would have remained all my life the sixth form [twelfth grade] student who wants his essay to be better than others and to be read aloud in class.

That's craftsmanship, always taking pains, never letting yourself tolerate less than your best.

Look now at the social aspect of our responsibility in the arts. This has two sides—the personal side and the wider one. As for the personal side, did you ever realize how much artists need other people? Common to them all is a basic desire: "I want my art to be used because it is for others. I want my pictures to be looked at, I want my music to be heard, what I write to be read, the play I'm in to be seen." Art, though a personal expression of talent, is also for others. As Peter said in the passage I've already quoted, "Each one should use whatever gift he has received to serve others, faithfully administering God's grace in its various forms."

There's a splendid give-and-take, a beautiful fellowship in Christian responsibility in the arts. Doing art is a lonely business—the performer's solitary hours of practice, the writer alone at a desk struggling with ideas, the painter or sculptor by himself in the studio. But once something is accomplished, there comes the reaching out to share it with others.

To turn your back on this reaching out is a denial of love toward your neighbor who wants to share his gift with you. To do that not only contributes to the frustration of God-given talent; it may also stultify our own capacity to appreciate and enjoy art. Full Christian responsibility in the arts entails a tolerance of and openness to all kinds of art, with only one exception—the kind that's corrupt. Take, for example, such contemporary forms as folk music and those aspects of jazz and rock and the new electronic sounds that are engaging the attention of many musicians. I don't claim to understand them, but I'm impressed that some musicians of great Christian integrity like Ray Robinson, president of Westminster Choir College, are telling us that there are in them possibilities for what he calls "a new synthesis of culturally reflective art with inherent value and a dynamic Christian message."

Fear of what's new can cripple Christian responsibility in the arts. Life in the arts as everywhere else means growth, and talent now, as in the past, has to launch out in new directions. The open mind, open eyes, and open ears in the arts are part of our artistic stewardship.

But there's the wider side of the social aspect of Christian responsibility in the arts. There's the question of what happens through group participation in them. Consider what can happen to an audience. They can be uplifted or debased together. Start at the highest level—worship. As a body of people we can be ennobled in a very special way as our hearts and minds are fixed on God and his truth and redeeming love. Without question art in the service of God can help uplift us in this way.

At the end of World War I, there was a great Jubilee Service in Royal Albert Hall in London. An American clergyman, Joseph Fort Newton, was sitting on the platform next to George Bernard Shaw. After the vast audience of thousands had sung from the bottom of their hearts Isaac Watts's hymn, "O God, Our Help in Ages Past," Shaw, deeply moved, turned to his friend and said, "I'd rather have written that hymn than all my silly plays." A new dimension of worship and uplift had come through the participation of all those people in the noble words and music of the hymn—a dimension beyond that of one's singing it alone. Similarly, it is rewarding to read *Hamlet* or *Othello* by oneself, but when we see them performed in public then we have the higher and wider experience of being caught up with others in their greatness. Or the play may be a comedy. Then there's the joyful experience of the group laughing together. Recreation, play, fun—these are part of the joy of art.

But suppose the play is rotten and depraved. Then you have the audience united in being debased. As Paul said at the end of Romans 1 after describing the sins of the pagans, "They not only do them but," as the New English Bible translates it, "they actually applaud such practices." And that's the ultimate degradation.

How do we discharge our Christian responsibility in this broader way? We can do it by being sensitive to the direction, morally and spiritually, that what we are seeing and hearing in the company of others is pulling us. This doesn't mean being prudish; the Bible has its dramatic portrayals of awful sin, as do the great dramatists also. Yet they deal with evil so as to sober us and warn us without pulling us down. The arts can be wonderfully interesting and exciting because they can bring us into our own personal encounters with greatness. Sometimes these happen through the help of a good teacher, sometimes through a friend, sometimes without any human intermediary. When this occurs I believe the Holy Spirit, who is involved in everything true and beautiful that happens to us, has his share in it.

Finally, Christian responsibility in the arts means that we always have to criticize ourselves. The arts can, as we've seen, be deeply absorbing and captivating. They are among God's best gifts. But we who work in them and live with them must be very careful that they don't completely take us over. If that happens, we confuse the gift with the Giver himself and that's idolatry.

The one great motivation for our Christian use of the arts is that which was so beautifully exemplified by that most Christian of musicians, Johann Sebastian Bach, who wrote on his works "Soli Deo Gloria" and meant it because he wanted God and God only to have the glory in everything he did. The apostle Paul put it in even greater words when he wrote to the Christians in Corinth, "we take captive every thought to make it obedient to Christ." That's the final word on Christian responsibility in the arts and, indeed, on the whole of life.

The Debasement of Taste

*T*o the American mind censorship is abhorrent. Unlike the totalitarian state, ours is a country in which men may speak, write, and publish as they wish and read and see what they want. Just as governmental requirements of religious and political conformity are intolerable, so censorship in literature and in the visual and performing arts is repugnant to our society. To be sure, there are legal limits to the exercise of free speech and artistic expression; the law prohibits obscenity that is utterly without social value, malicious libel, and subversion of national security amounting to "clear and present danger." Yet we seem in principle to be moving toward a position in which it will be increasingly difficult to define and enforce the limits beyond which the spoken and written word and the various modes of artistic expression may not go.

Thoughtful observers of American society can hardly fail to recognize the almost Copernican revolution that has taken place in American standards of decency. What was a trend two or three decades ago has in the last five or ten years become a landslide. The daring plays or pictures of the late fifties seem tame in comparison with today's "adult" entertainment. That a

109

minister of a great denomination should place on the pulpit alongside the Bible a book denied free circulation since the eighteenth century because of its salaciousness ought not to be considered merely an individual aberration but should be seen for what it is—one of many signs of a changed climate of opinion that now stomachs what only a few years ago would have been spewed out as morally defiling. Of recent years the public sense of propriety has been chipped away under the ceaseless impact of literature, entertainment, and advertising that have gone further and further in unending exploitation of sex.

To turn to another field, the unanimous decision of the Supreme Court throwing out a $500,000 award in an Alabama libel suit against *The New York Times* has upheld the right of criticism of public officials (even though the criticism may be false) provided that it is not made "with actual malice." The decision was doubtless necessary; in a democracy political discussion must at all costs be kept free from reprisal. However, two justices, Hugo L. Black and Arthur J. Goldberg, in concurring opinions, in which Justice Douglas joined, advocated the removal of the qualification regarding malicious intent. Justice Black's call for "granting the press an absolute immunity for criticism of the way public officials do their duties" was consistent with his statement in 1962 that any and all libel and slander laws along with any prosecution whatever of spoken or written obscenity are ruled out by the First Amendment.[1] Though few would go so far as this, it is evident that the widening interpretation of the constitutional privilege of freedom of speech and the press carries with it a heavy obligation of self-restraint.

Censorship, self-restraint under liberty, or untrammeled freedom of expression in speech, the press, and the arts— which? This is the problem. There are no easy solutions. And for this reason and because no problem comes closer than this one to the springs of human conduct and welfare, it must be the subject of deeper Christian thought and concern. Certainly the present situation in which almost anything can be said, written, or portrayed may yet result in a reaction that will impose restrictions in default of the exercise by individuals and groups of socially responsible self-restraint.

Further questions need to be asked: Is the public taste descending to a point of no return through mass media that reach as never before practically all the population? The licentious Restoration drama in England led to reform through the middle class; but what if the general standard of propriety has been lowered throughout society? Or, looking at the problem from another side, is it reasonable, while assuming on the one hand that the only truly effective censorship or restraint is self-imposed, to suppose on the other hand that man in his alienation from the God of holiness and truth will exercise such self-restraint?

To such questions there are no easy answers. But they must be asked; and as they are asked, the Christian position respecting the moral relativism of the day must be clearly and unashamedly stated. It is not the task of the church to impose its convictions upon the world, but it is the obligation of the church to declare its convictions to the world. In a day when multitudes have substituted a laissez-faire morality for the biblical ethic, Christians are responsible to live in a non-Christian world according to the teachings of their Lord and the Scriptures which testify of him.

This leads to the responsibility to practice Christian nonconformity in a society that is brimful of materialism and sensuality, and that widely repudiates the gospel with its ethical corollaries. And this in turn entails a Christian critique of cultural values, based not upon withdrawal or isolation from culture but upon compassionate understanding of it in the light of biblical revelation.

What, then, are some principles of Christian action in a morally corrupt society? Short of the millennium, Scripture knows no such thing as a Christian world order; with utter realism it sees the church and the believer as in the world and therefore with responsibilities to it but at the same time as generically different from it. As a new man in Christ, the believer has in spiritual reality an other-worldly origin, although he lives in a this-worldly environment.

The inevitable result is tension. "The world," said Christ of his disciples, "has hated them, for they are not of the world." What he stated with such profound simplicity is developed throughout the New Testament, especially but by no means exclusively in the Pauline epistles. But this polarity between Christians and the world does not exempt them from their continuing responsibility to be "the salt of the earth" and "the light of the world."

It is at this point of creative witness that ambiguities arise in respect to the Christian attitude toward the wide-open expression so characteristic of contemporary literature and the arts. Because these mirror the mood of the time with its restless search for meaning and escape by those who do not believe in the gospel, many Christians feel that we must know what is being communicated. And so we must—within limits.

"But what," it may well be asked, "are these limits?" Briefly they may be comprehended under three principles: that of Christian responsibility for the thought-life, that of Christian responsibility for one's brother, and that of Christian nonconformity to the world.

Individual responsibility for the thought-life is implicit in the Sermon on the Mount, in which Christ searchingly equates sin in thought with sin in act: "anyone who is angry with his brother will be subject to judgment . . . anyone who looks at a woman lustfully has already committed adultery with her in his heart."

To know what the world is thinking and saying does not mean willing capitulation to its obsessive preoccupation with illicit sexual activity. The argument that books such as *Fanny Hill* with their descriptions of prostitution and perversion provide a useful background for choosing virtue is as sensible as advocating visiting a brothel as an inducement to chastity. No Christian is obligated to reside in the brothels of the mind in order to know the world in which he lives. For those who feel obligated to know what people are reading, sampling under Christian conscience is sufficient acquaintance with the redundant portrayal of lust that fills so many pages and occupies such unending moving-picture footage. The inescapable principle that thought leads to action has not been canceled by dropping practically all reticencies in fiction and on the screen. It is still true that as a man thinks in his heart, so he is, and that "the pure in heart will see God."

"But what of the 'erotic' passages in the Bible?" To that question, frequently raised by defenders of morally questionable literature, the answer can only be that the attempt to equate the restrained way in which Scripture speaks of sex or the beautiful imagery of Solomon's Song with a *Tropic of Cancer* or any other scatological novel is sheer intellectual dishonesty convincing only to those who are ignorant of Scripture.

A second responsibility relates to one's brother. The glorious truth is that Christians have liberty of thought and action. They are under grace, not law. But their liberty has inherent limits. As the apostle shows in his classic exposition of Christian liberty in Romans 14, liberty may not be exercised in such a way as to "put any stumbling block or obstacle in your brother's way." No reasonable Christian would distort this principle to the extent of subjecting all literature and art to bowdlerizing; there must be a place for honest and responsible portrayal of human life in the actuality, often unpleasant, of evil as well as good. Yet Christians cannot in the exercise of their liberty escape responsibility for youth. If promiscuity is rife among adolescents throughout the country today—including many church-going young people—the question of where they learned their "new morality" is in part answered by what paperbacks and magazines they are free to buy at the corner drugstores, what they read even in respectable periodicals, and what they see in their neighborhood theaters as well as on the television screen at home. Indifference to human welfare when responsibility for others demands restraint of personal indulgence, is a mark of our age; and it shows itself in lack of concern for what is happening to children through debasement of public taste.

A third responsibility is that of nonconformity. Christian

protest is overdue. Making every allowance for contact with and understanding of the world, the call of both church and believer is to nonconformity. Paul's "do not conform any longer to the pattern of this world, but be transformed by the renewing of your mind," has ample roots in the teachings of Christ. Samuel Rutherford of seventeenth-century Scotland put the principle in vivid words, "You will find in Christianity that God aimeth in all his dealings with his children to bring them to a high contempt of, and a deadly feud with the world"—words that echo the drastic statement of James the brother of the Lord, "don't you know that friendship with the world is hatred toward God?"

What is needed is a resurgence of Christian responsibility expressed first of all in self-restraint and thoughtful discrimination of values. The wholesale avoidance of all modern literature and entertainment will not do. Not everything the world does is corrupt. Under God's common grace unbelievers write great novels and plays, paint beautiful canvases, compose fine music, and produce worthy motion pictures. Yet when the world uses its abilities to degrade public morality and debase human life, then Christians are obligated not only to nonconformity but also to open protest.

In *The Decline and Fall of the Roman Empire*, Edward Gibbon gives as one of the main causes of the growth of the early church in the decadent empire the pure morality of the Christians, who, by their steadfast nonconformity to the world around them, shone as lights in the darkness and worked as salt in a pagan society. The principle has not changed. Purity for conscience' sake, goodness out of conviction, self-restraint motivated by love for God and man, have not lost their winsomeness. In this secular society, as in imperial Rome, Christlike living still has its ancient power.

"The Debasement of Taste," Notes

1. Interview with Professor Edmond Cahn, *New York University Law Review*, June 1962.

PART 2

EDUCATION AND THE ARTS

Plan and Scope of The Stony Brook School

*I*n his able volume on the American secondary school, Professor Julius Sachs of Columbia University remarks that one of the chief services of the private school has been its ability to point the way toward newer and finer usages in education, to experiment along sensible lines.

Such a statement is particularly descriptive of The Stony Brook School. Except for the fact that we like to think of Stony Brook as something more definite than an experiment, Professor Sachs's words might be said to apply precisely to this school. The word *experiment* has acquired a rather unfortunate connotation, a connotation suggestive of uncertainty. And Stony Brook is more than an experiment as experiments are popularly conceived. It is an enterprise built upon the foundational truths of Christianity. These are the great and abiding things—the eternal verities. Our contemporary philosophy, a large part of our religious thought, is colored by the idea of relativism, the endless ebb and flow of things. Yet the great truths remain. They are immutable, abiding—as much more firmly fixed than the mountains as the infinite transcends the finite. They cannot be shaken; they constitute "the everlasting yea."

117

It is upon this rock that The Stony Brook School rests. And it is upon this rock that its future growth will be built.

There is a word that has been used extensively in the printed announcements of this school. It is a word happily chosen because it summarizes the essentials of the Stony Brook plan. That word is *correlate*. The central aim of this school is to correlate Christian principles, the great and eternal verities, with education of a type high enough to merit intimacy with such exalted ideals.

In a sense, this aim, this correlation, involves the thought of reconciliation. Our American public schools have tended toward the divorce of religion from education. This is a tendency in many ways unfortunate, but it is a tendency the basis of which is traceable to a great principle of our democracy—the separation of church and state. The gap between religion and common education spreads ever wider. In many respects, the two are now absolutely separate. Only in the Sabbath-school and in some of the private schools does the child receive definite religious training. And how slight this is! And how perfunctory it often is! And how few, comparatively, are the children who profit by it!

Education without character is a dangerous thing. For character, not intellectual agility, is the source of right living. But character itself has a source. It springs not from moral maxims, rules of conduct, proverbs, or thou-shalt-nots. Its derivation is higher. It grows out of religious experience—the effective religious experience that is the result of the gospel of our Lord and Savior Jesus Christ. This gospel is the only gospel that brings to the heart of him who accepts it that mysteriously beautiful change called regeneration—that mystic process that nurtures good deeds and godly character as certainly as the warm sunlight sprouts the seed in spring. Many schools boast that they build character. Diverse indeed are the methods which they employ to this end. We know that we are right in our emphasis upon the Christian gospel. We know that we have stricken at the root of character-building.

We find, then, these facts: education without character is worthless. Character is the wellspring of moral conduct. And character itself depends upon inspirational force. That inspirational force is found in the religious experience, and that experience, in turn, is derived from the Christian gospel.

The preparatory school standing, as it so often does, *in loco parentis*, is all powerful in molding character. During the critical years of adolescence, it creates the environment of the boy for three-fourths of each year. If the environment which the school creates is noncommittal on the vital matter of religion and of faith, the boys whom it turns out will also be noncommittal on these essentials. If the school is perverse in religious teaching, the morals of the boys will be warped. But if the schools hold forth as the great objective of human effort a fuller knowledge of God and an obedient realization of his plan for the individual life, it will send out boys anchored in a faith bearing the true source for right living. To achieve such an environment is the task of The Stony Brook School.

A word about specific details. How are we going to make actual our ideals? How give them a real and a dominant place in the life of the school?

As many of you know, the Stony Brook Assembly is founded upon seven principles that constitute a great reaffirmation of essential Christian truth. In its five principles for the Christian school, The Stony Brook School affords an analogy to the Assembly.

These are the principles for The Stony Brook School:

1. The Christian school must be comparatively small, with a correspondingly large staff of teachers.

2. The teachers in the Christian school must qualify as masters of their subjects.

3. The Christian school must maintain an atmosphere that is consistent with its aim.

4. Spiritual things must have their rightful place in the Christian school—and that place is the first place.

5. The Christian school must ever preserve a nice balance between the religious, scholastic, and recreative phases of its work.

Let us consider each of these principles very briefly.

1. The Christian school must be comparatively small, with a correspondingly large staff of teachers. True Christianity is contagious. It is caught more easily than it is imparted. More than any other faith, it is mirrored in the life of the believer. And in a school it must obviously be caught from the teachers, for they are the patterns for the students. The contact between the boy and his masters must be unusually close, closer even than in the usual private schools. This is why The Stony Brook School has a faculty of eight for its student body of twenty-seven boys.

2. The teachers in the Christian school must qualify as masters of their subjects. If this is true, the teaching will be of the kind that makes a genuinely deep impression. The boy who graduates from the Christian school must have full respect for the scholarship of his masters. Nothing is more dangerous to the faith of the youth than for him to make the disconcerting discovery that the men who have advocated his faith are men of mediocre ability. It was with this, among other things, in mind that the faculty of The Stony Brook School was selected.

3. The Christian school must maintain an atmosphere that is consistent with its aim. *Atmosphere* is a term often vaguely used. Yet atmosphere is one of the chief requisites for the successful school. Religious observances, prayer hours, chapel services, Sabbath-school, all contribute to the creation of the Christian atmosphere. Yet they are but the outward signs. Taken alone, they are apt to become merely perfunctory. Far more vital is the effect of personality. In the Christian school, every teacher, every employee, must be Christian. The combined personalities of school staff and student body must unite to create a spirit that is wholesome in its religion. Happiness, manliness, courtesy, sincerity—these are the characteristics that must be sought. Pietism, the "holier than thou" attitude, should have no place in an institution where boys are trained. For this reason, only men of dynamic Christian personality have been given places on the faculty of The Stony Brook School. And the student body has been drawn almost entirely from distinctly Christian homes.

4. Spiritual things must have their rightful place in the Christian school—and that place is the first place. The Bible must be at the center of the curriculum. Stony Brook has a special department of the Bible, supervised by an ordained minister. The course in Bible is a subject required throughout the five years of the curriculum. No student will be graduated unless he has earned a satisfactory rating in this course. And consequently no Stony Brook boy will be left ignorant of things essential to faith. Theology for theology's sake will not be taught. The inspirational value of the department will never be engulfed by the pedagogical point of view. Yet the influence of the Department of Bible must dominate; it must reach out and embrace all other courses. The masters in languages, in history, in sciences, must cooperate with the master in Bible. The pupil must be made to realize that his faith is an ancient faith. Through the thrilling story of the martyrs of the early centuries he can learn this. History can continue to show him such things as the strategic value of Wycliffe's work, the world changes attendant on the Reformation, and the fundamental bearing on the founding in America of the religious ideals of the Colonists. Study of English literature will reveal the transcendent beauty of the Bible and its tremendous influence on writers of all classes, from Chaucer through Shakespeare, down to Stevenson and Kipling. Work in modern languages will reveal the fact that the Scriptures are wondrously beautiful in all tongues. The ancient versions will be made an interesting part of the supplementary reading in Latin and in Greek. Science, taught from the Christian point of view, is a fascinating revelation of God. In this way, the whole curriculum can be made to revolve around the Bible with no sacrifice of proportion.

5. The Christian school must ever preserve a nice balance between the religious, scholastic, and recreative phases of its work. Religious observances and classroom work must never encroach upon the hours of recreation. Athletics and wholesome fun are essential. Just as much as any other boy, the Christian youth needs a sound body. The Christian school must have an

experienced director of athletics. Participation in some form of outdoor sport must be required of every boy.

In order to put these principles into practice in the most efficient way possible, the Christian school must be humanistic in the best sense of the word. For the Christian point of view is itself in essence humanistic. The fatal misconception of the scholastics of the middle ages, that Christianity is incompatible with liberal education, ought never to be revived. The greatest injury that the Christian institution can render to its faith is to fall, at this late day, into obscurantism. A humanism that would have every essential study taught in the most efficient way possible, that would never yield one jot in the field of scholarship; a humanism that, in its broad application, would help each individual student to solve his own unique intellectual and spiritual problems—this will guide the faculty of The Stony Brook School in their glorious adventure in Christian education—an adventure that will serve the church of Jesus Christ by conserving the faith of her youth, an adventure that will serve the nation by giving to it, year by year, a body of young men of stalwart character, well-taught and nurtured in the faith.

The Word of God in Education

A careful look at our subject, "The Word of God in Education," will provide a clue to the manner in which it ought to
be treated. Quite evidently, two things are placed side by side—
the Word of God and education—one in relation with the other.
The first of the two, "The Word of God," needs close definition;
the second, "education," must be brought to focus upon the particular kind of education with which we are here concerned,
namely, the Bible college or Bible institute. This is a specific
type of institution, to be sure, but the principles that will be discussed apply as well to other fields of education.

Consider the first phrase, "The Word of God." Though a
synonym for the Bible, this by no means exhausts the meaning
of the phrase. In a Supreme Court opinion, Justice Holmes once
wrote this sentence: "A word is not a crystal, transparent and unchanged; it is the skin of a living thought, and may vary greatly
in color and content, according to the time when, and the circumstances under which, it is used." Here we have one of the
first principles of exegesis of any book, the Bible included.

Viewed then in its scriptural usage as "the skin of a living
thought," we may identify three aspects of "the Word of God" in

its relationship to education. They are: first, the written Word of God, the Bible; second, the Word of God manifest in creation; and third, the Word of God incarnate in our Lord Jesus Christ.

We begin with the Word of God as Scripture. Among Christians in general and evangelical Christians in particular, the Word of God is synonymous with the Bible. The equation is fully justified because it is made again and again in the Old and New Testaments. Here, as the names "Bible college" and "Bible institute" imply, is the central point of integration. But why so? Why not theology, as in many seminaries? Or why not the officially sanctioned philosophy of a great doctor of the church, as in the Roman Catholic institutions with Thomism?

Before dismissing the question as being so obvious as not to require an answer, let us look beneath the surface to see some reasons why this Book, and no other, must be central in Christian education.

The first reason is the sheer, unapproachable greatness of the written Word of God. Considered just as a book, it holds the first place by reason of the criterion voiced in the classic treatise *On the Sublime,* in which Longinus declares, "That is really great which bears a repeated examination and which it is difficult or rather impossible to withstand and the memory of which is strong and hard to efface. . . . For when men of different pursuits, lives, ambitions, ages, languages, hold identical views on one and the same subject, then the verdict which results, so to speak, from a concert of discordant elements makes our faith in the object of admiration strong and unassailable." This is the doctrine of literary criticism known as the Law of Universal Consent and it applies to the Bible as literature. It is a fact that over and above any other piece of world literature from Homer down through Virgil, Dante, Cervantes, Shakespeare, Milton, and Goethe, no book has been more fully acknowledged as great simply as a book than the Bible.

Let no Christian educator ever apologize to the sophisticated of the educational world for such a designation as "Bible College." It should be for all who are committed to this kind of education a badge of honor. To take as the center of the curriculum the one book to which alone the superlative "greatest" can without challenge be applied—this is neither narrow nor naive. It is just good judgment to center on the best rather than the second best.

But there is a deeper reason why the written Word of God must be at the heart of our schools and colleges, and that is its authority as the inspired, inerrant Word of God. At this point plain speaking is in order. The current movement to express in contemporary, understandable terms the eternal verities of the faith, so that the people whom we must reach for Christ will know what we are talking about, deserves support. We should rejoice at the renaissance of good and enlightened scholarship among evangelicals which is sometimes called neo-evangelicalism. But at the same time we must not blink the evidence that there is current among some evangelicals a subtle erosion of the doctrine of the infallibility of Scripture that is highly illogical as well as dangerous.

It is illogical for this reason. We live in a day when archaeology has come into conformity with Scripture to such a degree that the number o f alleged discrepancies used by destructive critics of the past in their effort to discredit Scripture has been greatly reduced. Today scholars are writing such chapters as "Reversals of Old Testament Criticism" and "Reversals of New Testament Criticism" (see the recently published symposium, *Revelation and the Bible*). Those who over the years have held a suspended judgment regarding Bible difficulties, while still adhering to the inerrancy of the Book, have found question after question cleared up by new knowledge. Therefore, with all our openness of mind and emphasis on scholarship, we need to be careful to maintain the historic, Reformed view of a Bible infallible in the autographs (a view not to be equated with the dictation, mechanical theory of inspiration, but one held by our Lord and the apostles). And we need to maintain this position against neo-orthodox views of the Bible that may infiltrate even the Bible college and Bible institute. Let us by all means redefine and restate the evangelical position, but never at the cost of yielding any essential part of the authority of the Bible.

The second reason why Scripture must be at the heart of education concerns its indispensable critical function. In a day of debased values and satisfaction with the second- and even third-rate, education requires a standard and point of reference by which the cheapened standards of our day may be judged.

Writing at the beginning of the industrial revolution in England, the poet Wordsworth declared: "a multitude of causes, unknown to former times, are now acting with a combined force to blunt the discriminating powers of the mind, and, unfitting it for all voluntary exertion, to reduce it to a state of almost savage torpor." And he went on to speak of the literature of violence and sensationalism of his day. But now, under the impact of far greater changes and forces than any industrial revolution, and beset with the debasement of plain, everyday decency, this violent age in which we live has far more need of discriminating judgment than that of Wordsworth.

No other book can fulfill this critical, discriminating function like the Word of God. As the writer of Hebrews put it, "the word of God is living, and active. Sharper than any double-edged sword, it penetrates even to dividing soul and spirit, joints and marrow; it judges [Greek, *kritikos*] the thoughts and attitudes of the heart." In a time which Sir Richard Livingstone has rightly called "The Age without Standards," the Bible alone qualifies as the supreme critic of life and thought.

Dr. H. Langmead Casserly has called our world "The Bent World." The "bent" refers to the distortion of sin that stems from the fall and runs through all of life. And from this "bent" even Christian education is no exception. We do not always realize that this distortion affects areas of knowledge and education to different degrees. As Emil Brunner has pointed out, the twist resulting from sin is most marked in the humane subjects like theology, philosophy, history, and literature. It is less marked in areas like physics and chemistry, and in mathematics it approaches zero. Thus there is Christian theology, Christian philosophy, or Christian literature, but not Christian mathematics. It is in the humanities that the curricula in our schools and colleges have their strongest emphasis, and it is here that the critical, penetrating, revealing function of the Bible is most needed.

Now true as this principle is, in practice it needs care and courage. Let us in Christian education be fearless enough in our reliance on Scripture as the critic to subject even our cherished formulations of the Bible to its own divine, discriminating judgment. Let us see in searching scrutiny of the Bible that some of the neat and pat outlines and schemes we taught a former generation may need revision. For God has yet more light to break forth from his Word. Let us therefore seek to the glory of God to develop in our students a proper critical-mindness that subjects all the thinking and formulations of men to the ultimate principles and judgments of the divine *kritikos*, the Word of God.

Acts chapter 17 gives us a significant example of this function of Scripture. The Christians at Berea, we are told, "were of more noble character than the Thessalonians, for they received the message [in this case doubtless the *kerygma* or proclamation of the gospel] with great eagerness and examined the Scriptures every day to see if what Paul said was true." In other words, these Christians subjected even the apostolic preaching to the test of the Scriptures. And, it should be pointed out, there is an extension of this Berean principle beyond even doctrine. I am not saying that technical knowledge in science or any other field must be checked point by point with the Bible, but that in respect to ultimates, to the comprehensive frame of reference in Christ by whom (Colossians 1:17) "all things hold together," the Bible is the final critic.

There is a third reason why the Bible must be at the heart of Christian education. This relates to the all-important matter of knowing and finding the truth. The obligation to graduate men and women with some degree of literacy in fields of science and mathematics.

We look again at the phrase, "The Word of God," to see its third meaning. While the Bible is assuredly "the Word of God" and while creation is God's other book, the Word of God is something even greater than these. As every Christian knows to his soul's salvation, the Word of God is also Christ. To the first two meanings of the phrase, "the Word of God," he sustains an indissoluble and preeminent relation. In Hebrews 4:12-16, we see the writer's thought moving from what most commentators take to be the written Word, to the Son of God, the incarnate Word. The plain fact is that Christian education must always see the Bible not as an end in itself but as pointing to Christ who is its theme and subject from Genesis to Revelation.

The moment we lose sight of the fact that the incarnate Word, the eternal Son of God, is greater than and above the written Word, which with all its inspiration and infallibility is still a product of the Holy Spirit, we are in danger of bibliolatry. As Adolph Saphir said, "By bibliolatry I understand the tendency of separating in the first place the Book from the Person of Jesus Christ, and in the second from the Holy Spirit, and of thus substituting the Book for Him who is alone the light and guide of the church."

For a school to be called a college or school of the Bible is in itself no guarantee of power. It is even possible for the orthodox to become so devoted to technicalities of biblical scholarship as to lose sight of him whom the Bible is all about. Said D. L. Moody in his forthright way, "The key to the whole Bible is Jesus Christ. You remember that on the way to Emmaus with those two disciples, 'beginning at Moses and all the prophets, he [Jesus] expounded unto them in all the Scriptures the things concerning himself.' Notice those two 'alls.' The one theme of the Old Testament in type and prophecy is the Messiah; and the New Testament deals with his life on earth, and with the Church which is his body, and with his coming glory."

When the Bible is really at the center in education, the one chief subject is not just the Bible in its linguistic and historic or even doctrinal sense. It is, over and above this, Jesus Christ. As Professor T. W. Manson remarked in a comment on Ephesians 4:20 (where Paul says by way of exhortation, "You have not so learned Christ"), "The writer speaks of learning Christ as you might learn algebra or French. It is an extraordinary statement and one, I think, that goes to the heart of the matter." Spencer Leeson, Bishop of Peterborough in England, in his Bampton Lectures at Oxford, titled *Christian Education,* heads his chapter on "The Content of Christian Education" with the eighth verse of Hebrews 13: "Jesus Christ is the same yesterday and today and forever." And how does a Bible college or any educational institution teach Christ? In the classroom, yes, but also by the kind of administration and teachers it has. By its ethical, disciplinary, and social tone, and by all that it is and stands for, it teaches Christ.

In conclusion, consider the implications of what we have been discussing. The implications for the Bible college, as well as for all Christian education, commit us in one direction, namely, toward the continuing obligation of excellence. At the Fiftieth Anniversary of the Cum Laude Society in 1956, one of the country's distinguished educators, Dr. Claude Fuess, Principal Emeritus of Phillips Academy at Andover, Massachusetts, spoke on the subject, "The Curse of Mediocrity." In his comment on the prevailing satisfaction with the average and second rate in our schools and colleges, he quoted this evaluation: "Dismal and hopeless mediocrity is the most serious menace to present-day primary and secondary education in America." And we might add, it is the most serious menace to college education also. If mediocrity will not do for public and secular education, it is doubly a curse, even a scandal, for evangelicals contentedly to tolerate it in education that is committed unreservedly to the Word of God with all the depth of meaning that accompanies such commitment.

Someone will say, "But we in Christian education just do not have resources in equipment and endowment that secular institutions have." That is true. In this world's goods Christian education is comparatively poor. But good taste and excellence and high personal standards and lofty intellectual achievement are not confined to the rich. Granted that the quest for excellence is a continuing one and that humility forbids anyone a feeling that he has arrived, the Bible college, along with every other part of Christian education, cannot evade the unremitting pursuit of excellence to the glory of God.

Hudson Taylor once said: "Every work for God has three states—Impossible, Difficult, Done." Most Christian schools and colleges have been through the "Impossible" stage, when it hardly seemed that they could ever begin. All of them are in the "Difficult" stage right now, and here they stay; to make the Word of God central in education, and to do this without mediocrity and with a growing attainment of excellence, is a day-by-day adventure. Only at the final time of accounting, when we stand before the throne of him whose Name is called "The Word of God," will "Done" be written over our endeavors to make the Word of God the center of education.

Schools and Arts, a "Creative Outburst"

*E*ven a brief survey of the far-reaching effects of the Reformation on education and the arts must recognize its antecedents. For one thing, the Reformation was closely related to the Renaissance. While Luther's testimony at Worms was, as Carlyle said, "the greatest moment in the modern history of man," it was also the culmination of the spiritual ferment of the several centuries preceding Luther, Calvin, and the other Reformers. Nor may the results of the Reformation be confined to Protestantism; they are found as well in Catholic thought and life.

Two great principles were basic to the influence of the Reformation on education and the arts: the final authority of Scripture, and the priesthood of the believer.

For Luther and his colleague Melanchthon, who had so much to do with education in sixteenth-century Germany, it was a spiritual necessity for the individual to read the authoritative Word of God. Therefore, great numbers of elementary schools were needed—a requirement called by Professor William K. Medlin of the University of Michigan "the most important educational development in European history since ancient times." And such it was, because in the long run it led to public schools.

The other principle, that of the priesthood of all believers, led in the same direction, for it "took the responsibility for education out of the hands of the priestly hierarchy and, practically speaking, placed it upon the rulers and ultimately upon the people."[1] Luther himself wrote in his "Sermon on the Duty of Sending Children to School" (1520): "I maintain that the civic authorities are under obligation to compel the people to send their children to school. . . . For our rulers are certainly bound to maintain the spiritual and secular offices and callings, so that there may always be preachers, jurists, pastors, scribes, physicians, school-masters, and the like. . . . " In all this, Melanchthon was at one with Luther, and so extensive were his educational endeavors that he "provided the foundation for the evangelical public school system of Germany."[2] Melanchthon also profoundly influenced secondary education through what he did in shaping the German "gymnasium" and was instrumental in the development of the university throughout Protestant Germany.

Aside from insisting with Luther on the responsibility of secular authority for education and the necessity of educating all children (and Luther was far ahead of his time in providing for the education of girls as well as boys), Melanchthon held a concept of an integrated Christian education similar to that which has recently been rediscovered by Protestant educational philosophers, evangelicals not least among them. He "put into the curricula of his schools, especially the higher schools, those subjects which would contribute most to an understanding of the Scriptures"[3] and justified the various subjects, including physics and astronomy, by their relation to God. His was an integrated curriculum, centering in the principles of "back to the sources" and "knowledge of Christ."

But the educational influence of the Reformation spread far beyond Germany. Along with the Lutheran there is the Calvinist influence. Like Luther, Calvin was committed to the extension of learning. Calvinism affected education in the Netherlands, where the Synod of Dort in 1618 required every parish to furnish elementary education for all and where the Protestant

Christian school reached its fullest flowering and set the pattern for the Christian day school movement in America. In Scotland the educational impact of Geneva came through Knox, and in 1646 the Parliament required a school in each parish. Education in France and Switzerland was mightily affected by the Reformation. "No one," said Calvin, "is a good minister who is not first a scholar." In an essay entitled "The Reformed Tradition in the Life and Thought of France,"[4] Emile Cailliet stresses the essential democracy of the French Reformed movement: "The new Christian learning stayed in close contact with the people. In France as in Geneva, every Reformed church was bound to have a school. Mothers would learn to read so that they might be the first Bible teachers of the children. . . . It was a Protestant, the philosopher Pierre Ramus, who at the time of the Renaissance organized higher education in France." Moreover, in the nineteenth century many French Protestants were educators, Guizot being a pioneer of the public school system.

To be sure, educational progress under the impetus of the Reformation was not an unbroken development. There were setbacks and lapses into formalism. But the indestructible seed had been sown.

Americans are well acquainted with the fruition of that seed. At its beginnings in the Massachusetts Bay Colony, education in this country was rooted in Puritanism. That our colleges and universities and also our free schools are generically among the educational fruits of the Reformation is not arguable. If America has the most extensive system of education the world has known, this is in large part the result of the Reformation. According to the distinguished educational historian, Edward P. Cubberly, "The world owes much to the constructive, statesmanlike genius of Calvin and those who followed him, and we in America probably most of all."[5]

Even so rapid a sketch of the educational results of the Reformation as this would be incomplete without some reference to Roman Catholicism. To the extent that the Council of Trent was the result of the Reformation it may be said to have influenced the improvements in Catholic education. Loyola and his followers assimilated into their own Jesuit system the best educational thought of the time, borrowing ideas from the College of Guyenne (headed by Cordier, Calvin's teacher), the colleges of Geneva, and Johann Sturm's school at Strassburg.

Through all the ebb and flow in education since the sixteenth century, the most productive event was Luther's translation of the Bible into the vernacular. Setting the pattern for the German language, it also reached far beyond the confines of Germany. (William Tyndale, whose translation contributed so much to the King James Bible and who had visited Luther at Wittenberg, was greatly influenced by Luther's German Bible.) Among Luther's highest achievements was his giving the people God's Word in their everyday speech. And it was Calvin who went on to develop from Scripture the great system of Reformed doctrine.

Let these things be kept clearly in mind, as our survey moves from education to another field. For the recovery of the Bible and the priesthood of the believer are at the roots of the influence of the Reformation in the arts as well as in education.

Two of the greatest arts—music and painting—must suffice to illustrate the aesthetic results of the arts. Luther himself was a good musician. Through his emphasis upon the use of the chorale and through liturgical changes, he gave Protestant worship the inestimable gift of congregational singing: "Luther provided for liturgical forms that gave the congregation opportunities for direct participation in the service."[6]

In his love for music, Luther was a true child of sixteenth-century Germany, which was "bursting with song." Zwingli, who was also a musician, banned music from the church as unworthy of sacred use. But Luther knew better. "The devil," he said, "has no right to all the good tunes," and his view prevailed. Calvin was not himself musical. Yet contrary to uninformed opinion, he did not object to the use of music by Christians but considered it among "the excellent gifts of the Holy Spirit." In the Reformed tradition, the use of music was narrower than in Lutheranism; yet it had its place, chiefly in the musical setting of the psalter. And the Church is permanently indebted for some of its enduring hymns ("Old Hundredth" among them) to such a composer as Bourgeois, who lived and worked in sixteenth-century Geneva.

If Calvin's attitude toward music has been misunderstood, that of the Puritans has been slandered. In a definitive study, Percy Scholes, whom the great musicologist Alfred Einstein calls "an unimpeachable British witness," has demolished the persistent misrepresentation that the Puritans hated music.[7]

But to speak of Reformation influence in music is to bring immediately to mind that most towering of musical geniuses, Johann Sebastian Bach. Bach was no isolated phenomenon. He came from a family so musically eminent that in Erfurt musicians were known as "Bachs," even when no members of the family were there. He also had great Protestant predecessors, such as Buxtehude and particularly Schutz, who wrote some of the most spiritual of all music.

Bach is the man who in a single work, *The Well-Tempered Clavichord*, "opened up all the wealth of later music, with its absolute freedom of key change," and who in his church music, notably the B minor Mass (a thoroughly Lutheran work, the form of which makes it impossible to use in the Catholic service), the St. Matthew Passion, and the cantatas, expressed the essence of the Reformation faith. The historian who said that in the course of three hundred years only one German ever really understood Luther, and that one was Johann Sebastian Bach, may have been guilty of a degree of overstatement, but he came close to the heart of the matter.

To trace the influence of Bach in musical history would require calling the roll of the great composers who succeeded him with the possible exceptions of Gluck and Berlioz. Although Bach was far from unknown to his major successors like Mozart and Beethoven, it was Mendelssohn who had much to do with the rediscovery of his choral music. At the age of twelve, Mendelssohn read an autograph of the St. Matthew Passion in the Royal Library at Berlin and did not rest until years later he had given the work its first performance since Bach's death. Thus wide recognition of Bach's church music came late. Today this music still stands supreme. At the heart of this supremacy is the man himself, the devoted Lutheran Christian, who could not view the passion of Christ as a spectator but only as one who was personally related to the Lord whose suffering he so poignantly portrayed in tone.

Side by side with Bach stands another great Protestant musician, Handel. Professor Carl J. Friedrich of Harvard says, "The crowning glory of baroque music, in which it reaches the pinnacle that transcends all limitations of period and style, was achieved by Johann Sebastian Bach (1685-1750) and Georg Friedrich Handel (1685-1759). . ."[8] It was Handel who took the oratorio, which had originated during the Catholic Reformation in the Oratory of Philip Neri in Rome, and made of it such a glorious work as the *Messiah*, the libretto of which is derived in every detail from Scripture. Different from Bach in the acclaim that came to him during his lifetime, which was largely lived in England, the man who wrote the *Messiah* could say that he hoped to die on Good Friday that he might rise with his Christ on Easter Day. Among the successors to his biblical oratorios, which also include *Israel in Egypt* and *Samson*, there stand Mendelssohn's masterpieces, *Elijah* and *St. Paul*, as well as many later works, such as Stainer's *Crucifixion*.

The chief glory of later Protestant music is the *German Requiem* of Johannes Brahms, a convinced Lutheran, of whom one biographer says, "The Christian teaching which he received from Pastor Geffcken, who prepared him for confirmation, laid the imperishable foundations of his love for old Protestant church music and its uncorrupted original melodies."[9] "People do not even know," Brahms once said, "that we North Germans long for the Bible every day and do not let a day go by without it. In my study I can lay my hand on my Bible even in the dark." Thus it is not surprising that for his Requiem Brahms himself chose the Scripture passages.

The Protestant spirit in music has many manifestations. Yet whether it be in the religious masterpieces of Bach or Brahms, or in the less-known treasures of Moravian music rediscovered within recent years in the United States, the devotion to

Scripture and the sense of the believer's priesthood that are at the heart of the Reformation find musical expression. For the deepest strain in Protestant church music is that of spiritual inwardness.

These same principles carried over into painting, where they brought a new measure of freedom. The magnificent achievement of the great Italian Renaissance masters has enriched humanity, and the world can only be grateful for their work. Yet their art was largely aristocratic rather than of the people. It portrayed the Christ, the Virgin, and the saints with the utmost mastery of line and color. And perhaps some of it also tended to a kind of artistic docetism in which the essential humanity of Christ was submerged.

But the Reformation was not aristocratic. Nor did it encourage the Church to dominate art. In Protestantism, gorgeous ritual and the churchly display of magnificent painting gave way to the direct access of the believer in all his weak and fallible humanity to the Lord who was true man, "in all points tempted like as we are, yet without sin." Thus the Reformation, particularly in its Calvinistic phase, worked in painting to free it from the patronage of the Church and to make it more accessible to all men everywhere (see chapter v of A. Kuyper's *Calvinism*, the Stone Lectures for 1898 at Princeton Theological Seminary).

The tendency to bring Christ close to man in the reality of his divine manhood is evident in such works as the *Crucifixion* by Matthias Grunewald, the most powerful of all portrayals of Christ's suffering. Standing on the threshold of the Reformation, Grunewald shows with unforgettable pathos that it was man as well as God who hung and suffered on the cross. In her book, Jane Dillenberger says of this picture, "The miracle is that through the intensity of physical suffering speaks the atoning sacrifice of 'the Lamb of God who taketh away the sin of the world.' . . . The early years of the Reformation and the early twentieth century [Rouault] have both given us notable images of a Christ who died in order that the Christian believer may live and die in him."[10]

The most representative of all German artists, Albrecht

Durer, spanned the transition from the Renaissance to the Reformation. He himself was deeply committed to Luther and his
cause, and he "might have become the artist of the Reformation
had not death intervened not too long after his crisis of the
spirit."[11]

But it is to the Netherlands, that most Calvinistic of Protestant countries, that we must look to find the painter who is the
epitome of the Reformed influence in art. That man is Rembrandt. From his mother he gained great familiarity with the
Scriptures. (One of his earlier portraits shows her reading her
Bible.) His small library of only fifteen books contained, according to the catalog inventory of 1656, "*een oude Bijbel*" (an
old Bible), in which he was deeply read. A man of the people
who was not always on good terms with his church, Rembrandt
reflects most profoundly the environment in which he lived. If
he was, as Paul Jamot says, "the most religious of the painters,"
it was because "he was religious and human at once."

It is perhaps not generally recognized that Rembrandt was
chiefly a painter of biblical subjects. His religious works greatly
exceed every other category, totaling 850, whereas the next
largest group (portraits) numbers about 500.[12] Furthermore, it
is significant that none of his commissioned religious paintings
was done for churches. They were essentially an "unchurched"
kind of religious art, presenting Christ for every man and thus
similar in spirit to some of the religious painting of our own day.
Not only did they have scriptural subjects; they also showed
deep insight into biblical truth. Rembrandt's portrayal of Christ
is far removed from the conventionalized and sentimental picture Protestant America seems to have taken for its own. Rather
is Rembrandt the graphic presenter of God's majesty and
Christ's tenderness. The Lord he depicts is "richly human. His
face seems worn and its expression is inward, as if the words
spoken were given rather than proclaimed. . . . The authority
with which this Christ teaches and proclaims the good news and
speaks of the forgiveness of sins is of divine origin. And yet he
is wholly human."[13]

Rembrandt occupies a place in painting comparable only to that of Bach in music. With him the Reformed tradition finds its deepest pictorial expression.

Music and painting are among the most subjective of the arts. By insisting that every man is a priest before God, the Reformation freed the individual Protestant musician and painter to participate in the creative outburst of activity loosed by the recovery of the Word of God for the individual.

"Schools and Arts," Notes

1. Clyde L. Manschreck, *Melanchthon: The Quiet Reformer*, 132.
2. Ibid., 143.
3. Ibid., 146.
4. *Theology Today*, I:349.
5. *The History of Education*, 332.
6. Howard D. McKinney and W. R. Anderson, *Music in History*, 302.
7. Percy Scholes, *The Puritans and Music in England and New England*.
8. *The Age of the Baroque*, 87.
9. Walter Niemann, *Brahms*, 182.
10. Jane Dillenberger, *Style and Content in Christian Art*, 149.
11. Roland H. Bainton, *Here I Stand*, 125.
12. Dillenberger, 194.
13. Ibid., 186, 187.

The Idea of Excellence and Our Obligation to It

*E*ducators have an innate fondness for slogans. "Educating the Whole Child"; "Educating for Life Adjustment"; "Educating for One World"; "Educating for the Space Age." So the slogans come and go. Most of them have had a real point to make, and our schools have doubtless been helped by considering them. All of them have faced the danger of wearing out into cliches. But excellence, the pursuit and practice of the best in teaching, this surely is a theme that we ought not let slip like the slogans of yesterday.

Let us, therefore, take a close look at "The Idea of Excellence." What is it? By what criterion do we determine the excellent, yes, even the more excellent, in our study and in our teaching? It is strange that in all the discussion regarding excellence, so little is said about the idea itself. Albert Einstein once remarked that we live in an age of perfect means and confused goals. This confusion relates to some extent to our thinking regarding excellence.

We all take for granted that there is such a thing. Like a shining thread it runs through educational thought from Plato, who defined education as the "training in excellence from youth upwards which makes a man passionately desire to be a perfect citizen and teaches him how to rule with justice," to John Gardner's recent book, entitled *Excellence*.

The fact is that the idea of excellence is a bit like the Greek god Proteus, who had, you will recall, the ability, when grasped, of changing into another form. John Gardner compares the word *excellence* to the Rorschach ink blot test in which each individual sees something different. And it is true that what each of us sees in the idea of excellence reveals much about him.

"But," someone persists, "what is excellence?" Well, the dictionary uses terms like these: "first-rate," "superior," "extremely good of its kind." In doing so it underscores something as important as it is obvious. Excellence is a comparative term.

As the first-rate, excellence stands over against the second-rate; as the best, it contrasts with the good or the better. If the idea is protean, it is because of the varying standards and differing points of view by which we judge it. Are we, then, forever shut up to relativism in respect to excellence? Are there no ultimates in the light of which our reaching for it may be assessed?

There is, I believe, an ultimate point of reference for the things that are excellent. We are not shut up to relativism. This becomes clear as we turn from the dictionary and from most educational writing to another source—namely, the biblical view of excellence.

Here is an idea of excellence that points away from us. It directs our gaze upwards and outside ourselves. Implicit in the biblical concept of excellence is the idea of transcendence. The words used have such root meanings as "height," "loftiness," and "majesty." In Scripture, ultimate excellence is seen as belonging not to men but to God, as in the description of him in Deuteronomy as the One "who rides . . . on the clouds in his majesty."

Such a point of reference is an exalted corrective to our human measures of excellence, necessary as they are to everyday living. What Plato pointed to in the Republic, when he declared, "Nothing imperfect is the measure of anything," Scripture makes plain. In his First Corinthian Letter, St. Paul speaks of some of his contemporaries who "measure themselves by their own standards or by comparisons within their own circle, and that," he concludes, "doesn't make for accurate estimation." "No," he continues, we should rather "judge ourselves by that line of duty which God has marked out for us" (2 Corinthians 10:12, Phillips).

Now do not misunderstand me. There is a kind of comparison of one person with another, a considering of student achievement through marks, rating scales, and objective test results, that is essential to education. But necessary as all this is, it falls far short of the ultimate concept of excellence.

One of the Old Testament words for excellence has the two meanings of "rising' (in the sense of "loftiness") and of "pride," so reminding us that preoccupation with excellence only on the human level, apart from ultimate goals, has in it the seed of its destruction. Real competence in teaching, high standards, these qualities and others like them are expected of independent education. But there is a danger in being satisfied with these alone. As Dean Gordon of the Princeton University Chapel has said, "We like to think that knowledge saves, as will be stated in many college commencements in about two months. We are willing to gamble on the wisdom of this world. Yet," he continued, "intellectual excellence may be the means of our destruction."

Yes, there is a peril of pride to which we in independent education are susceptible. It is easy, as our standards rise, for us who are administrators and teachers to boast about the bright young people we teach. And who of us has not done this? We have our programs for the gifted, our honors courses, the newer mathematics, comprehensive language programs, and perhaps even programmed instruction, a euphemism for teaching machines. But in themselves these things are not enough. Having achieved them, should not our attitude be like that described in our Lord's parable: "We are unprofitable servants; we have done that which was our duty to do"?

Look again at our theme of excellence. I remind you that this means relating our teaching and learning to a dimension beyond that which is measured—and in its place validly so—by our human standards.

And now to the second part of our subject, which is "Our Obligation to Excellence." Let us look at this broadly and then personally. Our Christian schools and colleges are independent. This fact spells *obligation* in capital letters. Throughout the history of American education, and particularly in the earlier years of our country, Christian independent schools and colleges have been in the forefront of progress. But the day is past when we can claim to be superior academically to all of public education. With the development of secular and tax-supported schools and colleges, Christian education has been outstripped by secular education. And only recently have we been coming back academically into our own. But there is one great area in which the opportunity to strive for excellence is uniquely ours. And that area is the pursuit of excellence in its full spiritual and God-ward direction.

None of us should minimize the earnest efforts for moral training being made in some public schools and in some secular colleges. Yet the fact remains that it is the peculiar privilege, even the birthright, of independent Christian education to teach the Bible and the Christian faith just as fully and deeply as it desires. What does this say to us? Or better, what obligation does it impose upon us? Simply this: in a time when our very survival depends upon closing the gap between technological power and moral and spiritual restraint in using that power, we in Christian education have the obligation of commitment to truth in all that we learn and teach as well as the duty to point young people to the highest examples of excellence—namely, the most excellent of all books, the Bible, and the most excellent of all persons, Jesus Christ.

I know very well that this may sound old-fashioned to some of our secular colleagues. But let us not be intimidated by what C. S. Lewis calls the chronological fallacy, by which he means dismissing ideas and values simply because they are not new. The criterion of truth is not the calendar. Whether we reach the moon and beyond, whether or not life is discovered on other planets, truth and righteousness, the difference between the knowledge of good and evil, the eternal verities, do not change. The obligation of excellence in Christian education entails, then, commitment to the truth in all that we learn and teach. Without the recognition and practice of that principle, even the most doctrinally correct education will fail to reach full excellence. So we consider for a moment or two the all-important question of our attitude to truth.

There is a human tendency to be timid about the truth. To put it plainly, there are some—and they are in both camps theologically (liberal as well as conservative)—who are afraid of the truth. They suffer from a species of *aletheiaphobia*, to coin a word from the Greek. Now when an evangelical Christian is afraid of the truth, it may be because he has equated some particular formulation with final truth. Therefore, when he sees some newly apprehended scientific truth, some breakthrough into wider knowledge as a threat to the system to which he is committed, he may react in fear and sometimes even in anger. But as Plato said, "No man should be angry at what is true." And, we may add, the reason is plain; for to be angry at what is true is to be angry at God, for he is the God of truth.

On the other hand, those of more liberal persuasion theologically are prone to another kind of *aletheiaphobia*. Priding themselves upon their openness to everything new, they may see in old yet unwelcome truth a threat to their cherished ideas. Theirs is not so much the fear of the expanding aspect of truth as it is the fear of the particularity of truth. But the fact is that all truth, whether old and cherished or newly revealed, is of God. Let us welcome truth, and when we cannot understand all its implications, for this is an essential condition of our finiteness, let us be assured that there is no real inconsistency in the truth of God and that all of it is reconcilable in Christ.

What is our attitude to truth? Is it openness or timidity? Do we fear new truth or do we welcome it? Our answers to these questions reveal much about our attainment of excellence.

But hand in hand with this commitment to truth there is for Christian education that is determined to seek excellence the ongoing obligation to make the Bible and him who is its chief subject the living center of its entire program.

I believe that Christian education does the young people entrusted to its care a cruel disservice if, along with the great books that are part of our heritage, it deprives them of a careful, demanding study of the greatest book. There is a poignant entry in the journal of the brilliant writer, Katherine Mansfield, who died of tuberculosis at an early age and who came upon the Bible only in her mature life, never having read or studied it until then. "I feel so bitterly," she wrote, "that I have never known these writings before. They ought to be part of my very breathing."

Let us make sure that our Christian education does not withhold "these writings" from young people who need them perhaps more than any generation has ever needed them. If the Word of God is to be part of the very breathing of our youth, then it must be well taught to all students in the Christian school and college. Indeed, no matter how superior our work in science or the humanities is, without first-rate Bible teaching Christian education cannot really be excellent. And if Scripture is first among books, it is because its central theme is the Person who showed once and for all in human life the ultimate meaning of excellence. Excellence means commitment to the best to the extent of choosing it beyond the better. For me, and I believe for very many of us, the best is made known in the Person and words and, above all, in the saving work of Jesus Christ.

A leading characteristic of youth today is their search for meaning and identity in a confused time. Dr. MacLennan of Yale tells of a little girl in New Haven whose mother was worried because the child persisted in using wrong words in the Lord's Prayer. Her version began like this: "Our Father who art in heaven, how-do-you-know-my-name?" She was not so far wrong at that. She had the unconscious insight to want to know what youth—yes, all of us—want to know, that God is near and that he knows us by name.

W. H. Auden describes it in these lines:

> To be young means
> To be all on edge, to be held waiting in
> A packed lounge for a Personal Call
> From long distance for the low voice
> That defines one's future. . . .[1]

And the Personal Call, the only call that can satisfy the heart of youth, comes from him who said of himself, "He calls his own sheep by name."

"Our Obligation to Excellence." In its highest sense this is a personal call, a personal obligation. Goethe is said to have remarked that the spirit tends to take to itself a body. So the idea of excellence in education must be manifest in us—not only classroom teachers but administrators also—because principals and headmasters, presidents and deans, are also teachers, teaching by their attitudes and actions. The fact is that if we are in earnest about communicating excellence, we must practice it ourselves. But this is a costly matter. The price is high and it will not come down.

Look at several aspects of that cost. More excellent teaching in the context of this discussion costs submission through faith. It entails nothing less than individual commitment to the most excellent Person, Jesus Christ, as he is set forth in the most excellent Book.

But faith must be followed by works. What are the works that we who aspire to excellence in teaching must do? Well, they are those of the mind and those of the heart. It is obligatory for us to be intellectual persons to the glory of God, and it is also necessary for us to show genuine Christian concern for our pupils. Neither is easy.

To be an intellectual person is not just to be intelligent, not just to store up credits and earn degrees; it means lifelong devotion to the things of the mind.

What of our own individual program of studies? (I address the question to all of us, faculty as well as students.) Does it contain things that are hard? All of us must have such a program.

None of us is exempt from voluntary intellectual work, quite apart from graduate courses we may be doing. Before engaging a new teacher, I wish that I might look at his personal library, at the kind of books he has, and that I might find out whether they are read. Above all, I should want to know whether the Bible is a living part of his library.

Then there are the works of the heart, by which I mean the attitudes and feelings out of which we learn and teach. "And yet I show unto you a more excellent way." So St. Paul introduces the greatest of all poems on love. Here I speak especially to my teacher colleagues. More excellent teaching is teaching constrained by love—not sentimentality, but love that honors and respects and likes youth. One of our Eastern schools for boys, the Pingry School, which recently celebrated its one hundredth anniversary, has this motto, "Maxima reverentia debetur pueris." Translated freely it means "The greatest respect is due boys." Yes, and girls too, and college men and women. More excellent teaching demands imaginative concern that sees beyond youth to the mature man and woman. It costs in self-expenditure of time and effort.

More excellent teaching can be had at a price: going the hard way. For as Alfred North Whitehead said: "The art of education is never easy. To surmount its difficulties is a task worthy of the highest genius. . . . It is the training of souls." Few, if any of us, would claim genius. But we have something better. We have available to help us the greatest of teachers, if we will submit ourselves to him who is more than teacher, who is the Savior.

Excellence—more excellent learning and teaching. To move in this direction day by day is not a beautiful ideal and nothing more. It is a live option and it faces every one of us. Not that we shall ever fully attain it. There is only One who is wholly excellent. Nevertheless we must press on in our high calling. Whether we do this and whether we are willing to pay the price of excellence is by the grace of God our own decision.

"The Idea of Excellence", Notes

1. W. H. Auden, *The Age of Anxiety* (New York: Random House, 1947).

The Christian's
Intellectual Life

*T*he chief business of a college has to do with the thinking of its students. God created man to be a thinking being. The Bible recognizes the central importance of thought. It does not, of course, speak in terms of modern psychology. When it deals with man's most characteristic activity, it uses not only the word *mind* but also more often words like *heart* and *soul*. It tells us that we are made in the image of the only wise God, an image that, though ruined through the fall beyond our power to repair, is not beyond God's power to regenerate through the work of Christ.

In the Bible the thought life is decisive. Solomon says, "As [a man] thinketh in his heart, so is he" (KJV). And again, "Above all else, guard your heart, for it is the wellspring of life." Paul exhorts us not to be conformed to this world but to be transformed by the renewing of our minds; and he gives us the charter for Christian thought when he says: "Finally, brothers, whatever is true, whatever is noble, whatever is right, whatever is pure, whatever is lovely, whatever is admirable—if anything is excellent or praiseworthy—think about such things" (Philippians 4:8).

Blaise Pascal, certainly one of the most biblical of all the great scientists and philosophers, says in his Pensees, "Man is but a reed, the most feeble thing in nature; but he is a thinking reed. . . . Let us endeavour, then, to think well." In other words, one of the great marks of man's uniqueness is his God-given capacity to think. Consequently, anything that diminishes our thinking tends to dehumanize us through making us less than what God created us to be.

We ought, therefore, as partners in Christian education, to take seriously our obligation to live our intellectual life to the glory of God. For us who receive the Bible as the Word of God, who ourselves know the power of the Savior who died and rose for us, the Christian's intellectual life is not an optional matter. It is for all of us. It is a "must" for every believing student and teacher.

The Christian call to the intellectual life is not just to an elite, a chosen few. It is not merely for members of the scholastic honor society, or for the faculty. Said Sir William Ramsay, "Christianity is the religion of an educated mind." Observe that he did not say that it is the religion of a brilliant or a gifted mind. We are not responsible for the extent of our native intelligence but for the extent of our use of the ability God has given us. And in the Christian liberal arts college the talents of the mind must be developed into Christian intellect. There is, as Professor Jacques Barzun of Columbia shows in *The House of Intellect*, a crucial distinction between intelligence and intellectualism; the former is our native endowment in mental aptitude, while the latter is the use we make of our individual ability in helping to develop a cultural tradition.

So let us go on to see some of the implications of the development of Christian intellect. Consider its distinctive nature. We Christians are people of the Book, not just any book, but the Bible—the greatest, most beautiful, most profound Book in the world, on the truths of which the Christian college rests. Because this Book has to do with man in the entirety of his being, and because of our relationship to the living Lord who is made known to us through it, our intellectual life is much bigger than our reason alone. It embraces all of us, including our will and our emotions. Man is a unit; we cannot isolate and compartmentalize our faculties. As Dr. A. W. Tozer put it: "The Greek church father, Nicephorus, taught that we should learn to think with our heart. 'Force your mind to descend into the heart,' he says, 'and to remain there. . . .' When you thus enter into the place of the heart . . . it will teach you things which in no other way you will ever learn."

Look now at the scope of the Christian's intellectual life. The charge is often made that those of us who take the Word of God as our guide are bound to be restricted in outlook. To this the best answer is to turn back to Philippians 4:8 where Paul outlines the scope of our thought and urges us to "think about" (literally "ponder," "let your mind dwell on") six categories of things: those things that are "true," "noble" (honorable), "right" (according to God's requirements), "pure" (and remember that purity of thought comes from purity of soul), "lovely" (all that is beautiful), and "admirable" (before God and our fellow man). What horizons these six open up! They invite Christian thought to explore every aspect of truth to the glory of God.

Yet we must remember that our pursuit of truth entails an obligation of personal commitment. Just as we should say with Paul, "For me to live is Christ," so we must, as A. P. Sertillanges suggests, learn to say in every aspect of our intellectual life, "For me to live is truth"; for Christ is himself the truth. As he is revealed in his perfection in the Word, he is the ultimate criterion and measure of truth.

Now to live for the truth means to adopt a scale of values different from that which surrounds us. It was Archbishop William Temple who remarked, "The world, as we live in it, is like a shop window where some mischievous person has broken in the night to change all the price labels, so that the cheap things have the higher price on them and the really precious things are marked down." Why is there this twisting, this reversal of values in the world? One reason is the divorce in worldly thinking between truth and its ethical and spiritual implications.

One of the contributions of Christian thought to our times

must be the recovery of the ethical and spiritual dimensions of truth. No matter how great the prestige of a college or university, the search for truth merely on the level of the reason will not do. To hold truth in a moral and spiritual vacuum is not good enough. Thoughtful secular educators are beginning to see this. Witness these words of President John Sloan Dickey of Dartmouth College: "I believe we must at least redouble our effort to restore the relevancy of moral purpose as an essential companion of intellectual purpose and power in any learning that presumes to liberate a man. . . . There is simply no civilized alternative to having personal power answerable to conscience."

What Dr. Dickey and others like him are seeking—that is, the connection between intellectual and moral purpose—is at the center of our Christian heritage. Observe that Paul's pattern of the subject matter of our thought—the things that are "true," "noble, "right," "pure," "lovely," and "admirable"—is united throughout with ethical values.

But the Christian's intellectual life goes even deeper than this union with morality. It is at bottom a life of faith. Let us never make the mistake of thinking that faith is unrelated to knowledge and the development of intellect. In the deepest sense, believing is the door to knowledge.

The blind spot in the striving of the non-Christian mind for intellectual achievement lies in the incorrigible secularism with which it disregards faith. Secularism is, as someone has defined it, the practice of the absence of God. If it is our privilege as Christians to see where the world is blind, let us be very humble about it. Let us also be very sure that our intellectual life is infused with faith. For only the thinker who believes that God "exists and that he rewards those who earnestly seek him" uses his mind, as he ought, to God's glory.

The challenge of the Christian intellectual life is indeed great. But it is not an easy challenge. It costs to have a mind that is really dedicated to the Lord. The reason there are Christians who are not going on intellectually to the glory of God is not that they are dull or incapable of learning, but simply that they will not pay the price. And the price will not come down. It is nothing less than the discipline of self-restraint and plain hard work.

Dr. Allan Heely, distinguished headmaster of the Lawrenceville School, was once asked by a voluble lady, enamored of progressive education, this question: "What, Dr. Heely, is your ideal curriculum for growing boys?" He replied as follows: "Any program of worthwhile studies so long as all of it is hard and some of it is unpleasant." This was a severe but wholesome answer which applies in principle to the whole range of education on through graduate school. A great fault of education today is that much of it is too easy, and the fault applies to college as well as to grade school. No student will ever make sound progress in learning if he chooses courses merely because he thinks they will be easy. No Christian, however pious, will ever grow intellectually if he feeds his mind on trash, on the third-rate; if he never on his own reads some hard books, listens to some great and profound music, or tries to converse seriously about difficult subjects.

Turning from these things to the greatest Book of all, let me ask, What is the place of the Bible in our lives? Have we the fortitude to maintain inviolate a daily time alone with the Word of God? One may be an intellectual person without the Bible, but one will never be a Christian intellectual without it.

Finally, we grow in intellect in the broadest and deepest sense as we submit ourselves to our teacher. And who is that? As Bishop Stephen F. Bayne, Jr., said in a semicentennial address at the Kent School, "God Is the Teacher." In the Christian college—and herein lies the inestimable value of a committed Christian college—the living God is recognized as the source of all wisdom and excellence. And how does he teach? Let me say it reverently. God is not a progressive educator. He teaches us daily, as we pay the price of hard thinking. He teaches us through his Word. He teaches us through teachers who in turn are taught by him. He teaches us through the discipline of trial and disappointment and suffering, and through our successes too. But most of all he teaches us through our Lord Jesus Christ.

When God teaches us, he is always saying in and through and above whatever we are studying and learning for ourselves, or in the case of us teachers, what we are teaching others, "This is my beloved Son; hear him."

The intellectual life at its highest and best is above all else a Christ-centered life. It means having the mind of the Lord Jesus. It has a goal, the magnificent, lofty goal, as Paul said, of taking "captive every thought to make it obedient to Christ."

Like the high priest of Israel who had written on the mitre over his forehead, "Holy to the LORD," so the Christian student and scholar, dedicated to the intellectual life, must have written over his mind, "Holy to the LORD," as he seeks to ponder and dwell on the truth.

PART 3

MUSIC

In Behalf of Music

*T*hat there are gaps in the knowledge of the best-schooled of us is beyond dispute. No man can know all things; and even the educated man, the college graduate, to limit the term to a single class of the educated, is expected to be familiar with but a fraction of the world's wisdom. In medieval times, the student was ambitious to master all learning; today, such ambition would be preposterous. Important fields of human endeavor must necessarily be neglected. Otherwise, a skimming of surfaces, a mere dilettantism will supersede sound training.

The college course, with its Bachelor of Arts degree, stands for education in the "liberal arts"; and this education, variable as it is, includes always work in the literatures, both ancient and modern, mathematics, the sciences, history, and some of the fine arts. It is obvious that these subjects, different as they are in attractiveness, do not receive equal consideration either from teachers or from students. It is also obvious that the literatures receive most attention, and that certain of the fine arts are most neglected.

This is natural. Professional and business men have always outnumbered artists. And none but misguided enthusiasts would

159

want to force men to become artists. This is all very well; but that true understanding and intelligent appreciation of the fine arts should be limited to their actual practitioners is another and unfortunate matter.

I am going to use music for an example. My aim is chiefly to persuade you that this art, an art of the highest worth, is but vaguely appreciated and almost totally misunderstood by the American "cultured." I say "American" because the situation in foreign, notably European, countries is not similar.

Every college graduate (again I limit the term *educated* to this small group) has some knowledge and appreciation of poetry and the drama. Very few college graduates, however, have any but the most inadequate notions of the history, aims, or technique of music. This is a bald generalization. To demonstrate its truth we have only to imagine ourselves asking a college graduate two questions: First—"Are you quite sure that you know in what ways the work of Dante differs from that of Edgar Allan Poe?" He would undoubtedly consider mere intimation of such ignorance on his part bold effrontery, almost a personal insult, certainly a grave reflection upon the extent of his education. And he would be justified; were he unable to answer this question, he would not be a cultivated man.

But now let us say to him: "Are you quite sure that you know just how the work of Palestrina differs from that of Chopin?" If he knows anything at all about what we have asked him, he will answer proudly; he will be proud of knowing a fundamental in the history of a supremely great art. The chances are, however, that he will reply somewhat in this manner: "I am not very well versed in the intricacies of 'classical' music. Of course, I enjoy it." Then he will smile, and will be, perhaps, secretly pleased at his little phrase, "the intricacies of 'classical' music." Or he may become facetious at the expense of 'classical' music when compared with 'popular' music. Of his colossal ignorance of a noble art, he will be almost unconscious and utterly unashamed. Such is, among our educated people, the usual attitude toward musical knowledge.

This is to be deplored. The literature of music contains as great a measure of nobility and high beauty as the poems, dramas, or novels of Chaucer, Euripedes, or Balzac. And all this beauty belongs as much to education and to culture as poetry does. Aristotle thought music the most "imitative" of the arts, and for him, "imitation" was the index of true art. "In rhythms and melodies," he says, "we have the most realistic imitations of anger and mildness as well as of courage, temperance, and all their opposites." And again, melody, even apart from words, has an ethical quality. This is profoundly true. Bach is as spiritual as Milton; Beethoven has all the higher reality of Shakespeare.

Music differs from literature in that total ignorance of its medium does not prohibit enjoyment. A man must know how to read English in order to enjoy Spenser's poetry; he need not read music in order to enjoy Chopin. This, however, is but partial enjoyment; those who know precisely what Chopin meant to do in his polonaises, mazurkas, or etudes, and who are sensible of the great services he rendered to pianoforte technique, appreciate his music far more than those who listen unknowingly. And how much pleasure does a work like the Bach Chromatic Fantasy and Fugue give to the trained hearer! It is a composition of the greatest permanence and loveliness. Because Bach wrote it in the contrapuntal style, only a handful appreciate its beauties. Yet the fugue in music is scarcely a more technical and restrained form than the sonnet in poetry.

The taste of a concert audience may be measured by the amount of applause and attention which it gives to the greatest things in music. What is the taste of our American audiences? Joseph Hofmann in a recent number of *The Literary Digest* is quoted as saying, among other things, "I would never play a composition which I considered beneath the level of my art, though I have often, to my dismay, been forced to play programs not of the ultra-high standards I would have desired." Unfortunately only a handful of artists are in a position to say, "I would never play a composition which I considered beneath the level of my art." Most artists must play such compositions because their audiences demand them; trifles of sentimentality, pieces that parade virtuosity for virtuosity's sake, are invariably accorded the greatest plaudits. These are the things which, were we to seek parallels, would correspond to the novels of a Harold Bell Wright or to the acrobatics at a variety show. In themselves they are innocuous; in that they usurp attention belonging to great things, they are subtly dangerous. They succeed in this usurpation because the cultivated and the educated people, who constitute the bulk of the audiences at the better concerts, are appallingly ignorant of the truly fine in music. Musically, they are little more than barbarians.

This brings us back, once more, to the colleges, for they train some of the educated members of society. The educated are leaders; if they give to music its legitimate place, the others will follow—slowly, perhaps, but inevitably. I cannot forbear making mention here of Harvard; with her unique glee club, that seeks constantly the highest, with her choir, and with other similar agencies, she is definitely working toward a larger appreciation of the finest in music. But Harvard is the exception. The majority of the colleges offer a few musical courses; practically none require even a single such course. Is not a little understanding of music as essential to a truly liberal education as chemical theories, or trigonometry?

The scholiasts of the dark ages included music in their quadrivium which, with the trivium, made up the "seven liberal arts," the medieval curriculum. And at that time the art of music, as we know it, had but begun. Today we are heirs to the glorious creations of masters like Palestrina, Bach, Mozart, Beethoven, Chopin, Brahms, and Wagner; today music has a place in our curricula no larger than that of the occasional course in short-story writing or military tactics. While it has achieved for itself preeminence among the fine arts, its "academic standing" has correspondingly fallen. True, this "academic standing" has ceased falling. What is now needed, however, is a renaissance of music among all of the educated. For, just as much as poetry and the drama, music is universal property. It is not for the musician alone; it is for all who lay claim to knowledge. It is one of those things which Saint Paul exhorts us to "think on"— the true, the honest, the pure, the lovely, and the "things of good report."

Such is the place of music in higher education. The question which I leave with you is this: Shall an art so noble, so inspiring, and so truly productive of good as is music, be thus neglected?

Music in Christian Education

What kind of music has a place in Christian life? What kind of music belongs in the school program, in the home, in the church, in the recreation of Christians? The foundation upon which our thinking about answers to these questions must rest is this: All truth is of God. Therefore, music that has integrity is part of God's truth and belongs in Christian life. Truth is not confined to the spoken and written word and to such fields as mathematics and science; it relates to the arts also.

So we consider some implications, or variations, of the theme that music is a valid part of God's all-embracing truth. Chief among them is the need for breaking down the misleading distinction between sacred and secular music.

What, after all, is sacred music? According to common practice, it is music linked either to religious words or music written for religious use. Thus there are Christians who, while suspicious of all so-called secular music as worldly, attend with clear conscience performances labeled sacred concerts in which a good deal of third-rate, sentimental music has been baptized, as it were, by association with Christian verse; or in which tawdry, tasteless hymn arrangements, false to any real musical integrity, are deemed religious. But is the principle of sanctification by association a valid criterion for the distinction, so common in evangelicalism, between sacred or Christian and secular or worldly music? Certainly not. Rather the only defensible criterion of the fitness of music for service as a handmaid of the glorious truths of the gospel is its own inherent quality, provided that it meets first of all the test of truth.

"And what," someone asks, "is truth in music?" Now, it would be presumptuous to attempt anything like a comprehensive answer to this question. But we may at least point in the direction of an answer. Consider it negatively, first of all. Music that is pretentious, music that is vulgar, music that reeks with sentimentality, that shows off by resorting to empty, ear-tickling adornment—witness the so-called evangelistic style of piano playing—lacks integrity. As music it is not true, even though doctrinally it may keep the best of company.

But what, positively considered, are some of the elements of truth in music? Are they not honesty of expression, sincerity in the sense of avoidance of the cheap and contrived? Surely they also include such elements as simplicity and directness. But on the other hand they do not rule out either complexity or sophistication as opposed to artless simplicity. Bach wrote some enormously complex music, yet there is no higher musical truth than his. Honesty and integrity in music are not confined to the simple and naive.

In point of fact there is a vast body of music that has truth and integrity, yet is not fitted for church use, although Christians may enjoy it because it is part of God's truth. For example, the Chopin polonaises or mazurkas, beautiful as they are, do not convey religious feeling. They have a place in the Christian's enjoyment of music but not in church.

Is there, then, music that as music, quite apart from words or religious association, is compatible with spiritual worship? Surely the answer is a clear yes. Music is not spiritual only by association. On the contrary, there is music that is innately uplifting in its appeal. To be sure, it cannot by itself convey doctrine and thus is not specifically sacred or Christian, but in its feeling and in its effect it is spiritually elevating.

Not all of Bach's religious music was written for church use. Some of the preludes and fugues, such as the great E-major Prelude and Fugue in Book II of *The Well-Tempered Clavichord*, are deeply spiritual. Unquestionably many of Beethoven's slow movements, such as the wonderful Arietta and variations of the last piano sonata (op. 111), speak with a transcendental, almost heavenly voice. To make a very personal reference, one of my abiding memories is that of listening after my father's funeral to the Adagio of Beethoven's Violin Concerto. The Scriptures had indeed given me their unique comfort, yet music also spoke its lesser and wordless language of comfort. Mendelssohn's Reformation Symphony has its religious moments and not just because of the use of "Ein' feste Burg." But the Cesar Franck Symphony without any such reference is also religious, even mystical, in spirit. The firm majesty of Handel, so compatible with faith, is not confined to the *Messiah*. Witness the universally familiar Largo, which, though composed for secular use, has found such wide religious acceptance. Or take a piece like the brief Mendelssohn Song without Words, called "Consolation," which we have in some hymnals under the name "Communion"; or the Schumann "Nachtstuck," which we know as the tune "Canonbury." Granted that personal taste enters into comments like these, still the point is clear that there is a wealth of absolute music that in itself is conducive to worship.

My own feeling is that more of this kind of absolute music should be used in our churches, not self-consciously but unobtrusively. The question may sound radical, but is the practice of always printing on our church calendars the names and composers of preludes, postludes, and offertories a good thing? Certainly we desire to develop understanding of fine music. But a church service is not a course in music appreciation. We must be careful that in reaching out for a higher level of Christian music we do not foster what Don Hustad calls "spectatorism," in which the people look upon parts of the church musical service as a performance.

Consider an illustration from painting. A distinguished artist had finished a canvas of the Last Supper. All was done with great skill, and the chalice in particular had been portrayed most beautifully. As one after another of the artist's friends looked at the painting, they said, "What a beautiful cup!" Then the artist realized that he had diverted attention from the Lord. Taking his brush, he painted out the gorgeous chalice and substituted for it a more quietly beautiful but far less obtrusive one. So should it be with music in worship. It should not call attention to itself or monopolize the center of attraction that belongs to the Lord alone. And it may well be that the use, almost anonymously, of some first-rate music that, while unfamiliar, is in itself spiritual, will help the atmosphere of worship.

"But what about gospel hymns? Must all of our church music be classical?" The questions come out of a chief point of concern in evangelical Protestant worship today. Surely the answer is that when it comes to gospel hymns and their more formal companions, it is not a matter of "either-or" but "both-and." For the criterion for gospel music must be the truth just as the truth is the criterion for theology. Christians ought not to tolerate a double standard in worship—namely, zeal for the truth in doctrine and disregard of the truth in art.

God's truth is wonderfully comprehensive. Some of the truest music ever written, music of greatest integrity, is folk music. Think, for example, of the nobility of some Negro spirituals. It is a mistake to confine truth in music to the classical, to the sophisticated, or to the old. Christians ought not be suspicious of music just because it is new or unfamiliar. Our respect for the classics must not obscure the fact that good music is being written in our time. And there are gospel hymns—and the number is not inconsiderable—that in sincere, artless expression are honest music. They belong in our worship and education. Included among them are hymns like "What a Friend We Have in Jesus," "Blessed Assurance," or "Saviour, Like a Shepherd Lead Us," a tune, by the way, that Dvorak wove into the last movement of his Violincello Concerto.

One gets a little weary of extremists who say, "Away with gospel music; it's all trash"; or of those who say, "Away with all the older hymns; they're all staid, doleful, and joyless." The antitheses are false. Not all the old, standard hymns are staid and somber; and even the best denominational hymnals contain some hymns of negligible value that are hardly ever sung. As for classifying all gospel music as trash, this is nothing less than obscurantism. It is more difficult to be thoughtfully discriminating than to fall back upon sweeping generalization. Nevertheless, discrimination according to the truth is the only responsible answer to the tension between gospel and standard hymns.

In point of fact there is a far greater threat to the musical integrity of our evangelical worship and education than the gospel hymn. This threat is the invasion of Christian music by certain techniques of the entertainment world. With the almost universal use of TV, radio, and record players, the primary God-ordained center of education, the home, has been infiltrated by the musical devices of Hollywood and the night club. What does the habitual use of such music do in a home? The plain answer is that it debases taste and cheapens the gospel. The writer of the editorial in the September 16, 1961, issue of "The Sunday School Times" was absolutely right in his slashing attack upon the dressing up of gospel melodies in the garments of show business. If the state of music among evangelicals leaves a great deal to be desired, then records in which the precious doctrines of our redemption are unequally yoked with the movie-theater organ or sung in the mood of cocktail-hour ballads have much for which to answer.

As a matter of fact, some forms of jazz may have more musical integrity than this kind of Christian music. As Professor Wilson Wade of Dartmouth has said, there is a type of jazz that expresses honestly the spiritual lostness and rootlessness of modern man. And while evangelicals would dissent from his conclusion that the integrity of jazz in reflecting the predicament of man today entitles it to a place in worship, there are those who would think its use as a spiritual medium to be less questionable than that of some of the shoddy music that finds acceptance among us. Paul's exhortation "Don't let the world around you squeeze you into its own mould" (Romans 12:2, Phillips) is an aesthetic as well as moral imperative; and it applies as much to some of the music so popular among many Christians as it does to jazz.

Now we come to the heart of the matter, which is the formation of musical taste.

Permit me a bit of autobiography, if you will. It is my privilege to be the son of a great Bible teacher, one who stood firmly upon the Word of God and who preached the gospel wherever he went. Why am I a Christian today? Because of God's grace in using the witness of my parents in my home, the place where, as a small boy, I received Christ as my Savior. And why am I a musical person today? Again, because of my home. Among my earliest memories is that of hearing my father and my oldest brother playing Beethoven's Fourth Symphony in a four-hand piano arrangement. Or I recall waking up on one of the Sunday mornings when my father was not out preaching and hearing him play Mendelssohn. This was long before the days of radio and record players. Yet we had music in our home. My father and brother were not great pianists, but they loved and played good music. The formation of good musical taste depends on hearing fine music—not necessarily in great performance, for that was not nearly so available in my boyhood as it is now, thanks to long-playing records, but in constant hearing of great music even in an unskilled performance.

What of musical education in school and college? Here, too, the same principle holds. Whatever else we do, we must expose youth to greatness in music. Moreover, we need to tell them the difference between the good and the bad, between the worthy and the unworthy.

As headmaster of a school that stresses academic standards and college preparation in these competitive days, I deplore the imbalance of the curriculum in most of our schools. Music ought to be a major subject like English and mathematics. Yet even with the little time at our disposal some real exposure to greatness is still possible. At Stony Brook, aside from such activities as the chapel choir (which is one of our most respected extracurricular activities), the usual class in music appreciation, private lessons on various instruments, and a rudimentary band, we try to give all our boys some personal exposure to musical greatness. Each year the whole school of two hundred plus the faculty is organized for part singing. Through weekly rehearsals we learn some great music and sing it at public occasions, such as the annual academic convocation or the baccalaureate service. Thus, we have learned choruses from the *Messiah*, a "Gloria" from one of Mozart's masses, some Bach, and this year we are working on a chorus from Haydn's *Creation*. It is refreshing to hear adolescent boys humming or singing Mozart or Handel as they walk about the campus. Again, there is regular exposure to music of truth and beauty through daily and Sunday chapel, not only in the singing of fine hymns but also through the organ. Concerts for the whole school at which distinguished artists perform fine music are a part of our program. But one speaks of these things with humility, realizing how very much should be done.

The principle remains unchanged, whatever our situation. The key to better things in Christian music is the hearing of greatness in music not only in the day or boarding school, not only in college and seminary, but in church school also. Not even the smallest child may safely be fed a diet of musical trash.

Consideration of our subject would be incomplete without a final look at ourselves. The great principle, no Christian education without Christian teachers, applies just as much to the school musician as it does to the academic teacher. No one who does not love music and know it first hand can teach it with full effectiveness. No teacher of music in a Christian school or college, Bible institute, seminary, or church who is not himself a regenerated person, knowing through commitment of heart and life the living Lord, can teach music as an integral part of God's truth. Music is a demanding art. To achieve excellence in it requires hard discipline and unremitting work. Yet with all his devotion to it a Christian musician must keep his priorities clear.

God is the source of all talent. When he gives talent, including musical talent, he gives it, not to be made an idol, but to be used to his glory. You may remember how humbly Haydn summed up his musical life. "I know," he said, "that God appointed me a task. I acknowledge it with thanks and hope and believe I have done my duty and have been useful to the world." Music is indeed a great gift; but it is the Giver, not the gift, who must have the first place in the teaching and practice of music.

In his own account of his conversion, the church father, Jerome, who made the Latin translation of the Bible, tells of a dream that led to his conversion. He dreamed, he says, that he appeared before the Judge. Asked who and what he was, he replied, "I am a Christian." But he who presided said: "Thou liest, thou art a follower of Cicero, not of Christ." For Jerome was a rhetorician, and his consuming interest and first love was his study of Cicero.

So the Christian musician must take care that the art to which he is devoted does not usurp the place that belongs to the Lord alone. He must be a Christian first, which means that everything without exception must be brought into captivity to the obedience of Christ, who in all things, music among them, must have the preeminence.

Beethoven:
A Bicentennial Tribute

*D*ecember 16 marks the birthdate of a composer who stands at the summit of musical greatness. On that day in 1770 Ludwig van Beethoven was born in Bonn, Germany. This son of an obscure court musician became an artist whose influence and ability to express in music the whole range of the human spirit have rightly been compared with Shakespeare's in literature.

Of all the great composers none has had closer study than Beethoven, and of none do we have fuller information. His upbringing was sketchy; his education, except in music, was meager—a deprivation he suffered from all his life. At the end of his twenty-first year he settled in Vienna, where he remained until his death on March 26, 1827. The intervening years were filled with inward struggle and unremitting work out of which came some of the supreme masterpieces in all music.

Life was difficult for Beethoven. His contemporaries knew his worth, and by middle age his reputation was international. But his was a fiercely independent nature, fully conscious of his genius. Socially he was awkward, inept, and sometimes rude. He was often irascible and in his business dealings

173

at times unreliable, while in personal relationships he could be unpredictable. Yet behind his thorny exterior were noble simplicity of character and lofty idealism. He loved nature and delighted to walk in the woods and fields, jotting down themes in his sketchbooks, of which more than 5,000 pages survive. For the use and development of his genius he had a lifelong sense of responsibility to God.

The tragedy of Beethoven's life was an inner one. It centered in his deafness and in problems with his nephew. This boy whom he lovingly tried to raise as a son proved unworthy. Nor was the uncle, so different from such an ordinary youth, capable of understanding him.

The greater trial of loss of hearing began as early as 1798 (the year before the composition of the First Symphony), when Beethoven was twenty-eight, and it progressed relentlessly to the practically total obliteration of his hearing that shadowed his later years.

What this affliction meant we see from the "Heiligenstadt Testament," a kind of self-revelatory "will" addressed by the composer to his brothers in 1802 but not found till after his death nearly twenty-five years later. In it he explains: "Ah how could I possibly admit an infirmity in the one sense which should have been more perfect in me than in others, a sense which I once possessed in highest perfection. . . . O I cannot do it, therefore forgive me when you see me draw back when I would gladly mingle with you. . . . if I approach near to people a hot terror seizes upon me, a fear that I may be subjected to the danger of letting my condition be observed." He went on to tell how, when a companion heard in the distance a flute he could not hear or a shepherd's voice he was unconscious of, he was driven to the verge of suicide. "Only art . . ." he cried, "withheld me, ah it seemed impossible to leave the world until I had produced all that I felt called upon to produce. . . . Divine One, thou lookest into my inmost soul, thou knowest it, thou knowest that love of man and desire to good live therein."

It was Aristotle who said that "musical compositions are, in their very nature, representations of states of character." So this "testament" with its pathetic outcry is reflected throughout Beethoven's work as in the Appassionata Sonata or the first movement of the Fifth Symphony. Yet deafness did not master Beethoven. Out of his struggle with it came not only some of the most exuberantly joyous music ever written but also works of the serenity and supernal beauty that are unique marks of his genius. Thus the greater slow movements—for example those of the third, fifth, and ninth symphonies, of the Violin Concerto, of the last string quartets, and certain of the greater piano sonatas—these contain some of the most consoling of all music. And there are places in his work, like the Arietta and Variations of the final piano sonata, where his music soars to the gates of heaven.

Beethoven had learned, according to J. W. N. Sullivan in his study of the composer's spiritual development, to accept suffering "as one of the great structural lines of human life," and so he came to "that unearthly state where the struggle ends and pain dissolves away." As for his religion, he was baptized a Roman Catholic but had very little contact with the church throughout his life. On his deathbed he gladly received the sacrament. His notebooks and other writings, while not reflecting orthodox Christian doctrine, unmistakably reveal the central place his faith in God held in his life. Because he translated his Job-like experience into tone, musical literature has no more profound statement of the problem of suffering and its resolution than his. This is one reason his great works are so universal. Geoffrey Bull, the English missionary who endured the torture of Chinese Communist brainwashing, tells in his book *When Iron Gates Yield* how one day in Chungking, after his captors had taken away his Bible and he was facing death, the "Emperor Concerto" refreshed him as he heard the whole of it coming over a radio somewhere outside his prison room. Even there, Beethoven was speaking.

With all its sublimity, Beethoven's music is very human. He can celebrate the beauties of nature, and more than any other of the great masters, laugh with the gigantic, down-to-earth humor of his great scherzos or with the more delicate wit of some of the rondos or bagatelles. To a very high degree he exemplifies that indispensable element of great art—its incarnational relationship to our common humanity. And in his music a powerful mind is at work. For it is the combination of intellect and emotion that gives Beethoven his compelling force.

Some good music makes agreeable "background" listening. Not so with a large part of Beethoven's work. Its logic is so inexorable, its structure so strong, that it commands the attention of the musical hearer. Those who have been hearing and playing him for a lifetime (as I have been doing for close to sixty years) know the lasting quality of Beethoven's greater compositions, with some of which music has yet to catch up. As Igor Stravinsky, the distinguished modern Russian composer, says of the C-sharp minor String Quartet, "Everything in this masterpiece is perfect, inevitable, inalterable. It is beyond the impudence of praise." Indeed, Beethoven's influence on certain leading contemporary composers is profound.

Now some may say, "This is all very well for musicians. But what has it to do with us in a troubled age when so many are in spiritual and physical need?" This, of course, is a modern form of the old question of Tertullian, "What indeed has Athens to do with Jerusalem?"—a question that in some minds today still challenges the propriety of Christian involvement with culture. We may discern in Beethoven several answers to it.

For one thing, the life and work of this man stand as a signal example of God's sovereignty. All men's talents and gifts—for preaching or teaching the Word, for business or government, for science or art, for all the manifold aspects of human life—come from God. In his sovereignty he graciously gives gifts as he wills—the more ordinary talents to many and supreme genius to a very few like a Rembrandt, a Dante and a Shakespeare, a Pascal and a Newton. God makes no mistakes in exercising his common grace for our edification and enjoyment. He is the God of truth, and when, as with Beethoven and others like him, the genius he gives is used with utmost integrity, we do God no honor if we look down upon its products or take no interest in them. Great and noble art is not a frill, a spiritual irrelevancy.

Properly used it is a God-given means of refreshment and enrichment. It is as much a manifestation of God's wisdom and greatness as the majesty of the mountains, the vastness of the seas, or the glory of the heavens.

Consider next the providential aspect of Beethoven's life. "God," as Emile Cailliet says, "is the great Doer of the unexpected." As unexpected as lightning yet guided infallibly by the all-wise God is the entrance of genius into the stream of history. So with Beethoven. It was providential for music that this man appeared when he did. He was, as H. E. Krehbiel, one of the leading American critics, wrote, "a gigantic reservoir into which a hundred proud streams poured their waters, he is a mighty lake out of which a thousand streams have flowed through all the territories which the musical art has peopled, and from which torrents are still pouring to irrigate lands that are still *terrae incognitae.*"

It was also providential that deafness overtook Beethoven. The history of music has no more moving scene than the one in Vienna at the first performance of the Ninth Symphony in 1824. Beethoven stood in the center of the orchestra, ostensibly conducting. The members of the orchestra and choir had been told to watch him but not to follow his beating time. An ovation came after the scherzo. Yet the composer just stood there, quietly turning the leaves of his score. A singer plucked his sleeve and pointed to the wildly applauding crowd. No wonder there were few dry eyes in the audience.

Why did this have to happen to such a great artist? Why was he brought to such a pass that in his later years his only communication with others was through their writing in his conversation books? The answer is that, apart from the strange providence of his deafness, he might never have composed music like the Ninth Symphony, the last piano sonata and last quartets, and the *Missa Solemnis*. Also the great works of his "middle" period reflect his tragic problem. As Alexander Wheelock Thayer, the author of the standard biography, put it, "who can say that the world has not been a gainer by a misfortune which stirred the profoundest depths of his being and compelled the concentration of all his powers into one direction?"

Hearing is essential to performing and conducting music but not to composing it. Beethoven, who had great gifts as a virtuoso and conductor, might have gone on to a brilliant public career at the cost of some real loss of productivity. But the tragedy of deafness turned his genius inward with glorious results for music. "At its greatest," wrote Neville Cardus in the *Manchester Guardian Weekly*, "music, more than any other of the arts, has gone beyond the phenomenal to the noumenal universe. . . . It is a paradox—the less the musical imagination is obsessed literally by the promptings of the outer ear, the clearer becomes the significance contained within the notes. Beethoven deaf got as close to the Thing-in-Itself, to the revelatory point where notation ends and spiritual exploration begins, as mortal agency so far has been able to arrive."

But Beethoven would never have done what Cardus is speaking of had it not been for his unswerving dedication to his work. He never made his difficult temperament an excuse for not working. In a time when integrity is in short supply, even more than Milton in his blindness Beethoven stands as a supreme example of artistic integrity. His sketchbooks show how very hard he worked at revising and developing his themes and shaping the logic of his compositions. In 1815 he wrote in one of his notebooks. "If possible develop ear instruments, then travel! This you owe to yourself, to men, and to Him, the Almighty: only in this way may you develop once more all that has remained latent within you." And in 1818, about the time he began work on the *Missa Solemnis*, which he considered his greatest composition, he exclaimed, "Once again sacrifice all the trivialities of social life to your art! O God over all!" Such integrity in the use of genius to the glory of its great Giver deserves renewed recognition in this bicentennial year.

Why is Beethoven still, two hundred years after his birth, the most played of all the master composers? Those who know his music do not need to be told why. Those who are acquainted with little more of it than the three imperious eighth notes and the half note that open the Fifth Symphony may find the reason by listening to Beethoven.

Here, then, is a challenge for the reader who is uninterested in classical music. Take time from some of the television trivialities at which most people today look, and hear some Beethoven records or tapes—one of the symphonies, the "Emperor" Concerto, the Violin Concerto, or other of the well-known works. Better yet, hear Beethoven "live" at a concert. Or again, turn off the "background music" on your stereo and give your whole attention to Beethoven. As Donald Francis Tovey, the great British musicologist, said, "his music is edifying . . . a supremely masterly and hopeful criticism of life." And as you listen, and keep on listening, thank God for this man whose music speaks so eloquently of struggle with affliction, of the joy and humor of life, of sorrow and consolation, and serenity that surmounts suffering.

The Greatest of All Songs

*M*usic has been described as par excellence the Christian art. From the days of Palestrina down through Bach, Handel, Beethoven, Mendelssohn, Wagner, Liszt, and Brahms—the great masters have drawn some of their deepest inspiration from Christian sources. One has but to mention such towering masterpieces as Bach's *St. Matthew Passion*, Handel's *Messiah*, Beethoven's *Missa Solemnis*, Mendelssohn's *Elijah*, and Wagner's *Parsifal* to prove the point.

Professor Paul Lang, the French musicologist, has explained this affinity of music and Christianity by the fact that the Christian faith is subjective; though it finds outward expression, it begins with a deep, inner experience. So also music is one of the most personalized of the arts. At any rate, there is much in favor of giving to music the exalted title of the Christian art.

To go back to sources, ancient music occupies in the Bible a place greater by far than any of the other arts. One can in Scripture find references by the score to music, musical instruments, and especially to singing. Few but scholars of the text realize, for instance, that the returned prodigal heard a symphony, as the

Greek literally puts it, when he came back to his father's house. And as is always the case with Scripture, one can find even in the various Bible references to music some vital spiritual lessons.

There comes to mind, for instance, that beautiful word of the sweet singer of Israel in the 40th Psalm:

> I waited patiently for the LORD;
>> he turned to me and heard my cry.
> He lifted me out of the slimy pit,
>> out of the mud and mire;
> he set my feet on a rock
>> and gave me a firm place to stand.
> He put a new song in my mouth,
>> a hymn of praise to our God.

What is the greatest of all songs? It is not the art song, the glorious Lied of the German composers, or the flowing measures of Italian melody. Nor is it the heavenly harmonies of which Job speaks in those sublime words, "The morning stars sang together and all the sons of God shouted for joy." No, the sweetest song of all according to Scripture is, as David says, "The new song, a hymn of praise to our God." That is the song of heaven. In those beautiful visions in the Book of Revelation, the apostle John tells us that those about the throne of Christ the Lamb of God, "sang a new song: 'You are worthy . . . because you were slain, and with your blood you purchased men for God from every tribe and language and people and nation." And then, John adds, the refrain is taken up by ten thousand times ten thousand.

Thus music brings its tribute to the central theme of Holy Scripture—the redemption of lost men and women. Would you have a new song in your heart, the sweetest song of all the world? There is only one way to have it, and that is the simple way followed by God's children from time immemorial—the way of faith in "the one true God and Jesus Christ whom he has sent."

PART 4

LITERATURE

The Bible and the Christian Writer

A s we think about the Bible in relation to Christian writing, we must define Scripture in terms of the King James or Authorized Version. The literary influence of other translations through more than three centuries has been but a drop in the bucket compared with that of the King James Bible. Perhaps the Revised Standard Version or some other new translation may eventually supplant the King James Bible. If so, the loss from the literary point of view will be very great, as some versions of inferior nobility and vigor of language replace the book that is literature's chief glory.

Turning now to the Christian writer, we need first of all to look closely at the adjective, *Christian*. If we limit our discussion to the evangelical segment of Christianity, let us be careful to avoid any parochialism of outlook. Evangelicals are not the only Christians. There are those who share with us a firm belief in historic, supernatural Christianity, who worship Christ as Lord and Savior, who take a high view of Scripture, yet who may not use all our terminology and who hold a view of the church and of the ministry different from ours. They, too, are

Christians, and from some of them we have much to learn, especially when it comes to writing.

Let us grant that the writer whom we are considering is a Christian, a regenerated child of God, committed to the evangelical doctrines of Scripture. The question is, What do we really mean when we talk about a "Christian writer?" We might say simply that we mean Christians who write. That is much too broad a definition. The other day I asked the editor of a leading Bible study magazine, "What's the matter with Christian writing today?" His answer was candid, if not entirely elegant: "Most Christian writers," he said, "can't write. Many of them can't spell or punctuate. And a lot of them have nothing to say anyway." The plain fact is that not every Christian who writes is a Christian writer!

We must go on, therefore, to identify the Christian writer as a Christian who, being reasonably competent in the craft of writing, treats his subject in a manner that directly or indirectly reflects his spiritual convictions. He may be working in such fields as theology, biblical exposition, philosophy, or other areas closely related to the faith. Or he may be writing about so-called secular matters. Again, he may be practicing what is often called "creative writing," such as fiction or poetry. Whatever his subject matter, he is a Christian writer if the Christian world view, which is the world view based upon the Bible, is reflected in his writing.

This distinction is subtle but all-important. Reflecting the Christian world view does not mean conscious and obvious moralizing or, heaven forbid, labored preaching. It does mean that Christians, and certainly Christian writers, ought to have a God-centered view of life and the world. And it means also that this view of life, this *Weltanschauung*, to use the German term, is not held in a vacuum. Anyone, whether writer, teacher, or scientist, who has genuinely committed himself to the Christ who is the living God incarnate has made a decision that henceforth will color all of his work and all of his thinking. How far-reaching that decision is Browning tells us in "A Death in the Desert":

> I say, the acknowledgment of God in Christ
> Accepted by thy reason, solves for thee
> All questions in the earth and out of it,
> And has so far advanced thee as to be wise.

All writers must write from some particular point of view. And Christian writers ought to write from a God-centered, Christ-oriented, biblical view of life.

But at this point in our discussion we must turn back to the Bible. What is there about Scripture that makes it the one book of incomparable influence upon the Christian writer? First, the truth that the Bible reveals; second, the manner in which it states this truth. The two are organically related in that the second grows out of the first. To begin with, it is primarily the distinctive, biblical view of life and the world that influences the Christian writer. The major premise of Scripture is the living God. He is the God and Father of our Lord Jesus Christ. He is the God who, through his Spirit, inspired the Book. He is the God who, when he speaks in the Book, tells the truth. In the Bible, therefore, he tells the truth about himself and about man, sin, the world that now is, and the world that is to come. Thus the Bible presents a view of life and of the world distinctively its own and in a class apart from all other philosophies and all other religions. And this view the Bible equates with truth.

Next, turning to style and form, we find a correspondence with the content of Scripture. The Book that communicates truth speaks truly. The reference here is not the inerrancy of Scripture, important though that is. Rather am I speaking from the writer's point of view. Though we must always remember that our Bible is a translated book, it is remarkable how little fumbling for words the sensitive reader sees in Scripture. In its use of words, the Bible is the best model, because it speaks directly and truly; in it the right word is in the right place.

Think, for example, of the declaration of John the Baptist, "Behold the Lamb of God, which taketh away the sin of the world." Here is finality of expression. So also with the words of our Lord, "By their fruits ye shall know them," or "Come unto me, all ye that labor and are heavy laden, and I will give you rest." Go back to the Old Testament and there is the same rightness of expression, as in the psalmist's petition,

> Search me, O God, and know my heart:
>   try me, and know my thoughts:
> and see if there be any wicked way in me,
>   and lead me in the way everlasting.

Likewise with Job's great affirmation: "Though he slay me, yet will I trust in him." It was not without reason that the Greek rhetorician, Longinus, in his treatise *On the Sublime*, which, by the way, every writer ought to know, took as an example of sublimity in literature the words of Moses in Genesis: "And God said, 'Let there be light,' and there was light."

Now this quality of unerring choice of the right word in the right place carries over to the writer who is steeped in the Bible. In the Princeton University Alumni Bulletin (1 June 1956), there is a moving address by Judge Harold Medina on "The Influence of Woodrow Wilson on the Princeton Undergraduate, 1902-1910," a period covering the judge's own college years. In this address, Judge Medina says this of Wilson:

> But how he could talk! And we flocked to hear him. . . . At first we were fascinated by his perfect diction and the skill with which he chose just the right combination of words to express his meaning. Pretty soon it dawned on us that what he had to say was important. There was no mistaking his sincerity; he spoke with a singular intensity; he was always quoting from the Bible; and bit by bit he got his spiritual message over to us. . . .
>
> Moral principles, ideals, action, achievement, power; all these spelled out to us in the words of Christ, with continual emphasis upon unselfishness and sacrifice, the peace and good will to men which went beyond one's own borders and reached out to all mankind, and the unending fight against what he called "the thraldom of evil."

Here was a man who really believed in unselfish devotion to one's country, who was seeking, in the words he quoted from the Bible, to "prove what is that good, and acceptable, and perfect, will of God," and to lead us out of the wilderness into green meadows where ideals and principles were formulated and acted upon. This is what young people craved to hear in 1909, it is what they crave to hear now, and it is what they will always crave to hear.

Woodrow Wilson was not only a great president; he was also a great writer, a great Christian writer, if you will. And he was a great Christian writer in large part because of his intimate and continued use of the Bible.

In his *Aims of Education*, Professor Alfred North Whitehead has written what Sir Richard Livingstone of Oxford calls the greatest statement about education outside Plato: "Moral education is impossible apart from the habitual vision of greatness." Unfortunately, Whitehead lets us down as he points to the history and culture of ancient Greece and Rome as "the habitual vision of greatness." Certainly for the Christian writer, "the habitual vision of greatness" is not classical history and literature but the Bible, the Word of the living God. And a host of great writers rise up to prove this point.

The influence of the Bible upon our literature is inescapable. Think of Shakespeare, who in his thirty-seven plays alluded to fifty-four of the sixty-six books of the Bible. How many Christians today know their Bibles that well? There is Bunyan, who, with meager education and knowing little besides the Bible, produced the greatest allegory in the English language. Edgar Allan Poe, whose subject matter was far removed from Scripture, drew heavily upon it, as Professor Forrest of the University of Virginia showed in his fascinating study, *Biblical Allusions in Poe*. We think too of Lincoln, the writer of our most imperishable American prose. In his recent book, *A Clerk of Oxenford*, Professor Gilbert Highet of Columbia University has a fascinating essay tracing, line by line and phrase by phrase, the influence of the Bible upon the Gettysburg Address. And at that he misses the echo of the close of the eleventh chapter of Romans in Lincoln's climactic series of phrases: "government of the people, by the people, and for the people."

The most telling illustration of the inescapable influence of the Bible upon great writers comes from the poet Shelley. Shelley was expelled from Oxford because he wrote a pamphlet entitled "The Necessity of Atheism." In it he said, "The genius of human happiness must tear every leaf from the accursed Book of God ere man can read the inscription on his heart." Or, in less rhetorical language, "Man must tear up the Bible, if he would know himself." Just eight years later Shelley wrote his greatest prose work, the critical essay, "In Defense of Poetry." At its climax, this is what he said: "Their errors have been weighed and found to have been dust in the balance [an allusion to Daniel]; if their sins were as scarlet, they are now white as snow [almost an exact quotation from Isaiah]; they have been washed in the blood of the mediator and Redeemer [New Testament, evangelical phraseology]." The brilliant, unbelieving poet of the nineteenth century could not escape the Bible.

Now we come to the paradox of the Christian writer today. More than any other of his fellow writers, the Christian writer of our time is close to the Bible. His faith is a biblical one, so much so that he has been labeled bibliolater, biblicist, or literalist. The epithets may not be accurate, but they show that he is known for his closeness to the Bible. Yet in spite of this relationship to the Scriptures, evangelicals by and large are not writing well.

I happen to be associated with a book club that is committed to the policy of selecting for its members only evangelical writing of genuine worth. A survey of our selections since 1954 shows that a large proportion of them have been books from other countries—England, The Netherlands, Switzerland, Germany, and Australia. Indeed, if we had depended upon the writings of American evangelicals, we should have had difficulty in continuing. Not only that, but of the many books submitted to us for consideration, many are marred by careless writing.

To cite another example, a while ago I read Albert Schweitzer's autobiography, *Out of My Life and Work*. The difference, theology aside, between this book and one by an evangelical writer that I read at about the same time was as the difference between day and night. With Schweitzer I felt in touch with a distinguished mind; the other book, although well-intentioned, was flat and uninspiring.

It was not always so. A few generations ago, and in fact, even more recently, evangelicals were writing a great deal better than today. Nor need we go as far back as Bunyan. Take for example a man of more modest ability, the Princeton theologian Charles Hodge. This is the tribute *The Cambridge History of American Literature* pays him:

> There is a strange sublimity and extraordinary perspicacity about the style of Charles Hodge. It is not style at all. . . . Yet . . . few books open the mind on fields of grandeur more frequently than this systematic theologian. Its prose is not unworthy of being associated in one's mind with that of John Milton. Out of the depths this man cried unto his God and found Him.
>
> He writes with transparent sincerity. There is neither condescension not cringing. There is nothing left at loose ends. There is no sparing of thought. . . . He only claims to apprehend the Word of God.

Of more recent evangelicals there is J. Gresham Machen, a writer not inferior to C. S. Lewis in his lucid facility in handling ideas. The *Systematic Theology* of Lewis Sperry Chafer contains passages of genuine nobility and power, especially in his treatment of the Atonement. Samuel Zwemer, apostle to the Moslems, wrote with notable vigor. And the books of Robert E. Speer, another evangelical, contain some eloquent writing; while for simple clarity, there is the work of Harry Ironside.

But why are Christian writers not doing better today? To put it bluntly, there seems to be a short circuit between the Bible and most of our contemporary evangelical writing. We ought to be doing some of the best writing of the times simply because we are, of all writers today, nearest the Bible. But we are far from producing the best work. Why? Why is our supreme model, our authentic "vision of greatness," being thwarted in its communication, if not of greatness, at least of distinction to our writing? The answers are not easy. I suggest six reasons why present-day Christian writing seems to be so little influenced by the Bible.

First of all, can it be that in this busy day of radios, television, picture magazines, tabloids, condensed books, much traveling, and many meetings, we simply do not know the Bible as well as we think we do—or as well as our predecessors knew it? Yes, we use the Book for preaching, for reference, for proof texts, for help and comfort. But is not much of our use of Scripture for an ulterior purpose? Do we really know and love and read the Bible for its own sake? There is such a thing as living in the Word, making it literally the vital context of life and thought. Bunyan did that and God used him to write a book of incomparable power.

Some years ago Charles Grosvenor Osgood of Princeton wrote a little essay, "Poetry as a Means of Grace." This is what the Princeton humanist—and he is a Christian humanist—advises, after recommending an intimate acquaintance with any one of the great poets as an antidote to modern materialism:

> Choose this author as friends are chosen . . . think of him daily in odd moments. Read a bit of him as often as you can, until at least parts of him become part of yourself. Do not consult other books, or people by way of explaining him any more than you can help. Let him explain himself. What you thus come to know in him will every day seem new and fresh; every recourse to him brings forth new thought, new feeling, new application, new aspects of things familiar. He becomes an antiseptic agent against all the agencies that tend to make life sour, stale, and insipid.

Apply this counsel to the Bible, as Professor Osgood himself does. This is what we need—this kind of living in the book, if the Bible is to communicate power to our writing. But for it to do this the evangelical writer must know the daily discipline of the Word of God, or it will never be for him a means of grace.

A second thwarted biblical influence in our writing is this: Many of us are not bringing to the Bible a truly Christian education. There is within us a tension between the secular and the Christian world view. Even in Christian institutions, the secular frame of reference has crept in. Yet all truth is God's truth; the Bible knows no other truth but God's. But most of us at some time in our education have become habituated—perhaps unconsciously—to the false dichotomy between sacred and secular truth. Thus, not being fully committed to a God-centered world view, we have allowed the secularism in our thinking to offset to some extent the biblical view of life.

A third reason for the short circuit between Scripture and Christian writing may be the comparatively low estate of aesthetic appreciation among evangelicals today. Is it possible that debasing the aesthetic faculty in some fields affects it in other fields? Consider the third-rate music that we so often hear and sing in our services—the jingling, flippant choruses unequally yoked to the name and work of our Savior, the hymns dripping with sentimentality. Think of the lack of good taste in some public presentations of the grand truths of redemption. At the close of a recent telecast by a popular evangelical leader, viewers were urged to write in for fifteen-cent key rings with "a cute little cross" attached. What has happened to our Christian, let alone our aesthetic, sensibilities? There is artistic integrity, there is truth in art as in science, history, or finance. The tear-jerking religious tune is false, because musically it lacks integrity. The heart-rending sermon illustration that never happened in the first place, though all too often told by the preacher as though it happened to him, everything in our life and thought that savors of sentimentality and pretension—these too violate integrity. Do not be mistaken. The Bible knows what sentiment is; it is full of true and valid feeling, because it is par excellence the book of

the human heart. But the Bible never sinks to pretense and sentimentality. And when evangelicals traffic in these things, the
noble and wholesome influence of Scripture may be thwarted in
our thinking and in our words.

In the next place, the supplanting of sound values by the
world's methods of popularity and success may be clouding the
influence of the Bible upon our writing. This is a difficult problem. Christian writing needs the note of contemporaneity, but
never at the expense of truth and never at the price of debasing
the coinage of sound usage. Words are important. The right
word need never be irrelevant. It is doubtful whether the right
and the true word is ever the cliché of the popular, mass-
circulation periodical. Exactness in usage is no more equated
with stodginess of style than good taste with a dull, unattractive
format in our publications. In an article in the *Atlantic Monthly*
a few years ago, Jacques Barzun dissected the growing vocabulary of business and bureaucracy. Words like *processing* as applied to human beings and the pretentious business usage of *contract* came under his scalpel. Perhaps a similar deflation is due
some of the overworked words in our evangelical vocabulary,
so that some day we shall no longer have to read about ministers
"pastoring" churches and writers "authoring" books.

The foregoing is related to a fifth explanation of lack of
biblical influence upon evangelical writing today. It may be that
some of us have forgotten the scriptural principle of hard work,
resulting in the achievement of excellence to the glory of God.
As Solomon put it in Ecclesiastes, "Whatever your hand finds
to do, do it with all your might"—a saying that finds its New
Testament extension in Paul's advice to the Colossian church,
"Whatever you do, work at it with all your heart, as working for
the Lord, not for men," coupled in the same chapter with this
great criterion: "And whatever you do, whether in word or deed,
do it all in the name of the Lord Jesus, giving thanks to God the
Father through him." But this costs; it costs hard work, and the
price will not come down. Whatever we are doing as Christians,
whether it be writing or teaching or anything else, let us re-

member that nothing is ever too good for the Lord. On the title page of his autobiography, *I Remember*, Abraham Flexner, whose report on medical schools revolutionized the teaching of medicine in America, quotes Hesiod: "Before the gates of excellence, the high gods have put sweat. Long is the road thereto and rough and steep at the first, but when the height is achieved then there is ease, though grievously hard in the winning."

Still another reason for the comparatively low estate of writing among evangelicals may be an overconcern with the outward marks of scholarship. In recent decades a good many evangelicals have been among the "have nots" when it comes to recognized scholarship. Today we are concerned, and rightly so, with the growing prestige of evangelical thought. Thus, some who are writing in the more technical fields may be betrayed into a cumbersome vocabulary under the delusion that they are thereby being scholarly and profound. We may, however, safely leave that kind of style to theologians like Niebuhr and Tillich, both of whom excel in it. Instead, we should try to write clearly and incisively like Gresham Machen, or with the fluid lucidity of C. S. Lewis, neither of whom is ever obscure and both of whom are scholarly without pretense. Or more modestly, we may seek the unadorned simplicity of an H. A. Ironside.

Finally, consider a noble example of the Christian writer at his best, the greatest writer and theologian of the Reformation, John Calvin. Before his conversion Calvin was one of the most brilliant humanists of the Renaissance. In a biographical essay, "Calvin and Augustine," B. B. Warfield says:

> It is interesting to observe the change which in the meantime [i.e., after Calvin's conversion] has come over his attitude toward his writings. When he sent forth his commentary on Seneca's treatise—his first and last humanistic work—he was quivering with anxiety for the success of his book. . . . He was proud of his performance; he was zealous to reap the fruits of his labor; he was eager for his legitimate reward. Only four years have passed, and he issues his

first Protestant publication—the immortal "Institutes of the Christian Religion" . . . free from all such tremors.

He is . . . content that no one of his acquaintance shall know him for the author of the book. . . . He hears the acclamations with which it was greeted with a certain personal detachment. He has sent it forth not for his own glory, but for the glory of God; he is not seeking his own advantage or renown by it, but the strengthening and the succoring of the saints. . . . He has not ceased to be a "man of letters," . . . but he has consecrated all his gifts and powers . . . to the service of God and His gospel.

What we see in Calvin, thus, fundamentally is the "man of letters" as saint. . . . He was by nature, by gifts, by training—by inborn predilection and by acquired capacities alike—a "man of letters," and he earnestly . . . wished to dedicate himself as such to God.

"The man of letters as saint." It is an exalted ideal that we see in a man like Calvin, or to turn to our own American litera-ture, in Jonathan Edwards, whose literary eminence is so clearly recognized in the recent life by Professor Perry Miller. Verily, it is a great thing to be a Christian writer—a writer who tells the truth about God and his Son, a writer in whose work there is reflected even in a very small way the beauty and power of the Bible.

Encounter with Greatness: Bunyan's Pilgrim's Progress

Now we are going to think about one of the masterworks in world literature. Mark Twain once described a classic like this. It is, he said, "something that everybody wants to have read and nobody wants to read." Now whatever else may be said of it, *The Pilgrim's Progress* is an authentic classic, and John Bunyan, its author, was a man of genius. But it is also, on the part of many today, one of the most misunderstood of great books.

If I may go back for a moment to Mark Twain, here is his definition of the complicated musical form known as the fugue. He said that a fugue is a piece of music in which one voice after another comes in and one person after another goes out. Perhaps that is the way in which some people look at *The Pilgrim's Progress*. It's a book teeming with people. One after another Christian meets them on his journey, and they all have something to say. So, much as in the fugue, one voice after another comes into this book, and let us admit there are some readers who walk out on Bunyan or who would walk out on him if they could. They are the kind of readers who answered a poll conducted by one of the university presses back in 1950 on the subject of the most boring classics. *Pilgrim's Progress* was number one on the list. Yet it was in good company. *Moby-Dick* ranked second, and others among the first ten were *Paradise Lost*, *Don Quixote*, and Goethe's *Faust*. That was fifteen years ago and *Pilgrim's Progress* is still going strong.

Moreover, I am perfectly sure that it will be living long after those who voted it most boring are gone and forgotten. Just in case you are inclined to be among those who are bored by *The Pilgrim's Progress*, listen to this from one of the best of the recent studies of Bunyan, a book by Professor Henri Talon of the University of Dijon in France: "No intelligent reader has ever fallen asleep over *The Pilgrim's Progress*." Take warning, therefore, if you begin to get sleepy.

Let's not be too much concerned at the derogatory remarks we hear about *The Pilgrim's Progress*. There are reasons for them. For example, there is the low estate of contemporary theology. Only the other day I was chatting about Bunyan with Dr. Roland Frye, professor of English at the University of Pennsylvania. (He has, by the way, written an excellent study, entitled *God, Man, and Satan*, in which he discusses the theology of *Paradise Lost* and *Pilgrim's Progress*.) He told me that one of his students in a graduate course at Penn, a rabbi who is a university professor in Israel, said that where he lives they have a name for such things as the death of God theology we read about these days. The word is *chutzpah*, which means unbelievable presumption—the kind of presumption of the man who murders his parents and then, when arrested, throws himself on the mercy of the court because he is an orphan. Now it's perfectly obvious that many who have very little idea of Christian theology, who are thoroughly secular-minded, who never read the Bible, and who don't think that God and the gospel are really important can't muster much enthusiasm for a book rooted and grounded in God and the Bible and in salvation through Jesus Christ.

On the other hand, by no means all who have admired Bunyan have shared his theology. For example, there's George Bernard Shaw, who was about as far from evangelical Christianity as anyone could be. Yet in the Epistle Dedicatory to his "Man and Superman," Shaw compares Bunyan's characters with those of Shakespeare, and he does so very much to Bunyan's advantage. In case any of you have been looking down your noses at the way Bunyan's characters talk, listen to this from Shaw, who was one of the great masters of playwriting. "Only a trained dramatic speaker can appreciate the terse manageableness and effectiveness of this speech. [Shaw is speaking of the dialogue in *The Pilgrim's Progress*.] The sentences go straight to their mark; and their concluding phrases soar like the sunrise, or swing and drop like a hammer, just as the actor wants them."

Do you know what the key test of enduring greatness in literature is? It was formulated back in the early part of the Christian era by a Greek author known as Longinus, who wrote a famous treatise called *On the Sublime*. After pointing out that one cannot downgrade a great work of literature because it does not survive a first hearing, Longinus says: "that is really great which bears a repeated examination, and which it is difficult or rather impossible to withstand and the memory of which is strong and hard to efface. . . . For when men of different pursuits, lives, ambitions, ages, languages, hold identical views on one and the same subject, then that verdict which results, so to speak, from a concert of discordant elements makes our faith in the object of admiration strong and unassailable." This is certainly true of *Pilgrim's Progress*.

I have been asking friends if they have read this book. Answers are various, but a surprising number of them have read it and they are by no means all older people. For instance, a few weeks ago we entertained at dinner a young Pakistaní whom I met last fall when I was in Pakistan giving some lectures. He is now in this country doing graduate work. When I asked him, "Do you know *The Pilgrim's Progress*?" he replied, "Yes, I do. I read it at home in Urdu." The other day I asked the research department of the Library of Congress some questions about Bunyan's masterpiece. They told me that it has appeared in practically every known language as well as in many dialects—in Africa, Asia, Oceania, wherever tongues are translated. Publishers everywhere, they said, have printed it as it came into the public domain. As the all-time best seller it is second only to the Bible.

While the literature about Bunyan has slackened some-what in recent years, it is still very much alive. Among recent works I have noted are biographies, two novels based on his life, and an exhaustive study of *Pilgrim's Progress* by a well-known psychoanalyst, and of course, the inevitable new editions of *Pilgrim's Progress* that continue to flow from the press. Among them is a simplified and condensed version in modern speech. This last seems to me sheer impertinence—to take the writer who above all others achieved the greatest simplicity and try to simplify him. The justification of this sort of thing is the modern rendering of Scripture. But the Bible is a translated book, whereas *Pilgrim's Progress* is an original English work.

Let me share a remarkable answer to my question about *Pilgrim's Progress* given me by the distinguished scholar and philosopher, Emile Cailliet, one of the world's leading au-thorities on Pascal. Dr. Cailliet has been professor of French lan-guage and literature at the University of Pennsylvania and pro-fessor of philosophy at Princeton Theological Seminary. Here is what he told me: "In my own estimation, next to the Bible which is in a class by itself, Bunyan's *Pilgrim's Progress* rates highest among all classics . . . the reason I have to put *The Pilgrim's Progress* next only to the Bible is that as I proceed along the appointed course, I need not only an authoritative book of inspi-ration and of instruction; I need a map. We all do. My considered judgment . . . is that Bunyan's masterpiece has provided us with the most excellent map to be found anywhere. Why, having read and reread the book some fifty times, I *see* that map most vividly unfold under my gaze, in whatever place or situation I find my-self. What clearer answer could one find to his basic questions, 'What kind of place is this?' and 'What should I do in the situa-tion?' What more adequate climax to the human quest for truth?"

The other day I asked my secretary, who is in her early twenties, if she has read it. She has indeed and is now teaching it by flannelgraph to little tots of five and six in her Sunday school class, and they love it. What a book—the guide for a philosopher and a story book for children!

Books inevitably reflect their writers. Of few writers is this more true than Bunyan. Here was a man born into the lower classes in English society in the earlier part of the seventeenth century. He was not illiterate but had only the scantiest education and practiced the humble trade of tinker. In his teens he served in the army at the time of the Civil War in England. Returning from military service, he married at an early age. He spent his life in a small area in the English midlands at Bedford, and was for twelve years in prison, an incarceration he could have terminated if he had simply agreed not to preach. Yet with not a tenth of the education you have already had, he wrote a book that, in one of the most creative centuries of English literature, when Shakespeare was at his height, when Milton and Dryden and John Donne and many others flourished, ranks with Shakespeare and Milton and has probably been read by more readers than have read either of these giants. Nor is *The Pilgrim's Progress* his only work. Among his thirty-nine published writings, in order of time it ranks twenty-first. In fact, including his unpublished work, Bunyan produced about sixty works, among them one of the great spiritual autobiographies of all time, *Grace Abounding*, and another book, *The Holy War*, which, had he not written *Pilgrim's Progress*, would surely rank as the greatest allegory in the English language.

Now the strange thing is that little of the stirring history of the period during which Bunyan lived is reflected in his writing, aside from his army experience which provided him with some of his imagery. Nevertheless, Bunyan does reflect his times, for this was the age of Puritanism, when many were deeply occupied with their inner life. You probably know that there has been almost endless discussion about Bunyan's conversion, as he tells it in *Grace Abounding*. Some have called him a sick soul. Macaulay, in his famous *Encyclopedia Britannica* article, considers Bunyan's experience essentially pathological. However, there is another way of looking at this key experience which we need to understand if we are to enter into the spirit of

The Pilgrim's Progress. As more recent research has shown, Bunyan's spiritual struggle, although notable for its intensity and the clarity with which he set it down in *Grace Abounding*, was by no means unique. It follows the pattern of spiritual experience among the seventeenth-century Puritans. To say this is not in the least to detract from its reality and authenticity. Here was a man who trembled on the very verge of the abyss. But as Dr. John Brown, his greatest biographer, points out, he always held control of the citadel of his will. After a struggle lasting for years, he emerged an integrated personality in Christ, able to cope magnificently with life, to endure imprisonment and to write his great books.

Few of you may read *Grace Abounding*. But whether you read it or not, remember that this terribly lucid and unsparing account of a soul's travail, a book that ranks with the *Confessions* of St. Augustine and those of Jean Jacques Rousseau, provides the essential crucible out of which came the experience reworked by Bunyan's genius in his great allegory. If, as Wordsworth said, "there is in poetry the element of emotion recollected in tranquillity," *The Pilgrim's Progress* is essentially poetry. Had its author's struggle of soul been less fierce, the superb recollection of it, transmuted by Bunyan's genius, could never have been written.

I am not a professional English scholar, though I love English literature and studied it in college and graduate school. What I tell you about Bunyan and *The Pilgrim's Progress* represents the point of view of a headmaster recently turned editor and a writer of many years experience. It is also that of a Christian who, though with some difference of emphasis, shares by conviction the heart of Bunyan's theology which, after all, is the evangelical faith that has come down to us through the Reformation.

Speaking then from this non-professional point of view, I pass over the supposed sources of *The Pilgrim's Progress*. Here the specialists have been at work, it seems to me rather needlessly. Of course, *The Pilgrim's Progress* is by no means the first book likening the Christian life to a journey. Why try to establish literary sources for it when the idea of the pilgrimage is clearly found in two New Testament epistles—Hebrews and 1 Peter? But Bunyan's reading was necessarily so restricted, particularly during his twelve years in jail, that it seems rather fruitless to try to trace in detail the sources of his ideas and imagery, apart from Scripture which is, along with his own experience, without question his lone great source. Undoubtedly some of the current ideas of his time influenced him, such as those in the romances of chivalry he read before his conversion. After his book appeared, some said it was not his own. But this transparently honest man, who even put alongside the three Latin words in *Pilgrim's Progress*, "The Latin I borrow," was simply incapable of plagiarism. With this everyone agrees, even specialists who are inclined to see sources and unconscious borrowings where they may not really be.

What is *The Pilgrim's Progress*? The first and most obvious answer is that it is an allegory. And it is indeed an extended parable, full from beginning to end of symbolism. But as every thoughtful reader knows, the symbolism cannot be pressed too literally. By universal consent the greatest allegory in the English language, if not in any language, one reason for its supremacy is that it is not over-complicated as, for example, is Spenser's *Faerie Queen*. Paradoxically, its strength lies partially in the looseness and even the inconsistencies of the symbolism.

But the book is more than an allegory. It is also a novel. Quite different from the kind of novel we read today, it is yet genuine prose fiction of germinal and lasting influence. For Bunyan, along with Defoe, shares the parentage of the English novel. Again, the book has another side. It is superbly dramatic, so much so that parts of its dialogue would liven the stage. As such it is a gallery of portraits, many, though not all of them, alive as few fictional characters have ever been given life by any writer. Finally and most deeply, it is an exposition of theology according to the Scriptures and of life lived according to the Scriptures.

Join me now, if you will, in what is for me the most pleasant part of this essay—namely, sharing with you some aspects of the book I enjoy most and find especially impressive.

Surely you have noticed the difference between Part I and Part II. The first is a story or novel of action, strong and masculine. Christian's journey is a hard one. As another seventeenth-century writer, the Scotsman Samuel Rutherford, described the road through life, "All that came there found wet feet by the way, and sharp storms that did take the hide off their face, and found to's and fro's, and ups and downs, and many enemies by the way." Quite different in mood is Part II. It is a gentler book, befitting its leading feminine characters, Christiana and Mercy. Less dramatic than its predecessor, it has rightly been called a novel of manners. In it some of Bunyan's choicest characters appear, such as Lightheart, Old Honest, Mr. Fearing, Greatheart, and Valiant-for-Truth.

Another aspect I find appealing is the rightness of Bunyan's narrative. Events occur as they ought, or at least as the reader is led to feel they ought. This feature may be found in literature, but also in music. For instance, one hears for the first time a work by such a composer as Beethoven, and the inevitability of the melodies and harmonies, the utter rightness of the rhythm and musical phrases, give the impression of hearing what is already known. So with *Pilgrim's Progress*. There are surprises in the story, but somehow they are familiar surprises.

Sometime ago I was on a journey round the world. I saw things in Japan and Hong Kong, in India, Greece, and Italy, that looked like what I expected to see. But in the Holy Land it was different. There I saw things I had never seen before, yet they were utterly and deeply familiar with a familiarity that reached into my heart.

Now I grant you that this feeling about *Pilgrim's Progress* is by no means unrelated to one's own background and experience. But I rather think that even for those much less farther on in their pilgrimage than I am and with far less biblical and theological knowledge, there is something of this quality in the book. We read it and something says inside us, "This is right. This is the way it ought to be. This is the way it really is."

You see, I am going back to my philosopher friend's analogy of the map. Only this is a very special kind of map—a map in pictures vividly colored. Above all it is a living map. People step out of it and walk along with you and talk with you in your imagination and stay with you in your memory.

At the outset of Christian's journey from the City of Destruction to the Celestial City, this matter of lifelike vividness confronts us. He has cried out, "What shall I do to be saved?" and Evangelist has come to him. Listen to how Bunyan tells what follows:

> Then he gave him a parchment roll; and there was written within, "Flee from the wrath to come!" The man, therefore, read it; and looking upon Evangelist very carefully, said, Whither must I fly? Then said Evangelist, pointing with his finger over a very wide field: Do you see yonder Wicketgate? The man said, No. Then said the other, Do you see yonder shining light? He said, I think I do. Then said Evangelist, Keep that light in your eye, and go up directly thereto, so shalt thou see the gate; at which, when thou knockest, it shall be told thee what thou shalt do.

Robert Louis Stevenson called this kind of writing, "the highest and hardest thing to do in words." And John Bunyan does this "highest and hardest thing" over and over again. In a superb essay on *Pilgrim's Progress*, John Livingston Lowes, one of my teachers at Harvard many years ago, says of this quality in Bunyan: "It is easy to say what a thing is *like*, and thousands have the trick. Direct vision, with the power of evoking it in us, is the gift of few, and among them are the greatest. Bunyan has it, and it is with his unswerving intensity of vision that we see: 'Behold I saw'; 'I looked, and saw'; 'I saw also'; 'as I perceived'; 'I looked then, and saw'; 'So I saw in my dream.' It is no wonder that the pictures live and breathe."

Take another example of this immediacy of vision—the

episode after Christian has been persuaded by Worldly Wiseman to detour to the village named Morality where the house of Legality was:

> *Christian:* Sir, which is my way to this honest man's house?
>
> *Worldly Wiseman:* Do you see yonder high hill?
>
> *Christian:* Yes, very well.
>
> *Worldly Wiseman:* By that hill you must go, and the first house you come at is his.
>
> So Christian turned out of his way to go to Mr. Legality's house for help. But behold, when he was got now hard by the hill, it seemed so high, and also that side of it was next the wayside did hang so much over, that Christian was afraid to venture farther, lest the hill should fall on his head; wherefore, there he stood still, and wotted not what to do. Also his burden now seemed heavier to him than while he was in his way. There came also flashes of fire out of the hill, that made Christian afraid that he should be burned; here, therefore, he did sweat and quake for fear.

Or this key passage, at the very heart of the book:

> Now I saw in my dream that the highway, up which Christian was to go, was fenced on either side with a wall, and that wall was Salvation. Up this way, therefore, did burdened Christian run, but not without great difficulty, because of the load on his back.
> He ran thus till he came to a place somewhat ascending; and upon that place stood a Cross, and a little below, in the bottom, a Sepulchre. So I saw in my dream, that just as Christian came up with the Cross, his burden loosed from off his shoulders, and fell from off his back, and began to tumble, and so continued to do, till it came to the mouth of the Sepulchre, where it fell in, and I saw it no more.

Then was Christian glad and lightsome, and said, with a merry heart, He hath given me rest by His sorrow, and life by His death. Then he stood still awhile to look and wonder, for it was very surprising to him that the sight of the Cross should thus ease him of his burden. He looked, therefore, and looked again, even till the springs that were in his head sent the waters down his cheeks. Now, as he stood looking and weeping, behold, three Shining Ones came to him and saluted him with "Peace be to thee." So the first said to him, "Thy sins be forgiven thee"; the second stripped him of his rags, and clothed him with change of raiment; the third also set a mark on his forehead, and gave him a roll with a seal upon it, which he bade him look on as he ran, and that he should give it in at the Celestial Gate: so they went their way. Then Christian gave three leaps for joy, and went on singing.

And as Bunyan looks back, when questioned by Piety at the Palace Beautiful, to this central scene of the book, his recollection has the same directness of vision:

Piety. And what saw you else in the way?

Christian. Saw! why, I went but a little way farther, and I saw One, as I thought in my mind, hang bleeding upon a tree; and the very sight of Him made my burden fall off my back; for I groaned under a very heavy burden, and then it fell down from off me. It was a strange thing to me, for I never saw such a thing before: yea, and while I stood looking up (for then I could not forbear looking), three Shining Ones came to me. One of them testified that my sins were forgiven me; another stripped me of my rags, and gave me this broidered coat which you see; and the third set the mark which you see in my forehead, and gave me this sealed roll (and with that he plucked it out of his bosom).

What a description of hand-to-hand combat Bunyan gives us when Christian meets Apollyon in the Valley of Humiliation:

> But now, in this Valley of Humiliation poor Christian was hard put to it; for he had gone but a little way before he espied a foul fiend coming over the field to meet him: his name is Apollyon.

After the fiend assails Christian with words, the battle begins.

> Then Apollyon straddled quite over the whole breadth of the way, and said, I am void of fear in this matter. Prepare thyself to die; for I swear by my infernal den that thou shalt go no farther: here will I spill thy soul. And with that he threw a flaming dart at his breast; but Christian had a shield in his hand, with which he caught it, and so prevented the danger of that.
> Then did Christian draw, for he saw it was time to bestir him; and Apollyon as fast made at him, throwing darts as thick as hail; by the which, notwithstanding all that Christian could do to avoid it, Apollyon wounded him in his head, his hand, and foot. This made Christian give a little back: Apollyon, therefore, followed his work again, and Christian again took courage, and resisted as manfully as he could. This sore combat lasted for above half a day, even till Christian was almost quite spent . . .
> Then Apollyon, espying his opportunity, began to gather up close to Christian, and, wrestling with him, gave him a dreadful fall; and with that Christian's sword flew out of his hand. Then said Apollyon, I am sure of thee now. And with that he had almost pressed him to death, so that Christian began to despair of life. But, as God would have it, while Apollyon was fetching his last blow, thereby to

make a full end of this good man, Christian nimbly reached out his hand for his sword, and caught it, saying, Rejoice not against me, O mine enemy! when I fall I shall arise!; and with that gave him a deadly thrust, which made him give back, as one that had received his mortal wound. Christian, perceiving that, made at him again, saying, Nay, in all these things we are more than conquerors through him that loved us. And, with that, Apollyon spread forth his dragon wings, and sped him away, so that Christian saw him no more.

But there are many places where this power of putting the thing itself before us springs out of Bunyan's pages. The description of Vanity Fair is another. So is the trial of Faithful in Vanity Fair. And so also is the imprisonment of Christian and Faithful in Doubting Castle and their deliverance from Giant Despair and his wife.

Often Bunyan paints his pictures through dialogue. Do you remember the meeting of Christian and Hopeful with Demas?

Then Christian and Hopeful . . . went till they came to a delicate plain called Ease, where they went with much content; but that plain was but narrow, so they were quickly over it. Now, at the farther side of that plain was a little hill called Lucre, and in that hill a silver mine, which some of them that had formerly gone that way . . .
Then I saw in my dream, that a little off the road, over against the silver mine, stood Demas (gentlemanlike), to call passengers to come and see; who said to Christian and his fellow, Ho! turn aside hither, and I will show you a thing.

Christian. What thing so deserving as to turn us out of the way to see it?

Demas. Here is a silver mine, and some digging in it for treasure; if you will come, with a little pains you may richly provide for yourselves.

Hopeful. Then said Hopeful, Let us go see.

Christian. Not I, said Christian; I have heard of this place before now, and how many have there been slain; and besides, that treasure is a snare to those that seek it, for it hindereth them in their pilgrimage. Then Christian called to Demas, saying, Is not the place dangerous? Hath it not hindered many in their pilgrimage?

Demas. Not very dangerous, except to those that are careless. But withal he blushed as he spake.

Bunyan can not only make us see; he can also make us hear. Surely you must have noticed as you read it the sounds in the closing pages of Part I, the passage that for sheer splendor mounts up in one of the great crescendos in literature.

They compassed them round on every side: some went before, some behind, and some on the right hand, some on the left (as it were to guard them through the upper regions), continually sounding as they went, with melodious noise, in notes on high; so that the very sight was, to them that could behold it, as if heaven itself was come down to meet them. Thus, therefore, they walked on together; and as they walked, ever and anon these trumpeters, even with joyful sound, would, by mixing their music with looks and gestures, still signify to Christian and his brothers how welcome they were into their company, and with what gladness they came to meet them. And now they came at it, being swallowed up with the sight of angels, and with hearing their melodious notes. Here, also, they had the City itself in view, and

thought they heard all the bells therein to ring, to welcome them thereto . . .

Now I saw in my dream that these two men went in at
the gate, and, lo! as they entered, they were transfigured; and they had raiment put on that shone like
gold. There were also that met them with harps and
crowns, and gave them to them; the harps to praise
withal, and the crowns in token of honour. Then I
heard in my dream, that all the bells in the City rang
again for joy, and that it was said unto them, "Enter
ye into the joy of our Lord."

Let's look at another side of Bunyan's art for a moment or
two. Go back to the quality for which George Bernard Shaw so
highly praised him—the amazing ability to create characters
that speak in living dialogue. Before doing this, let me say that
not all Bunyan's characters achieve this. Some, such as Hopeful, don't quite step out of the pages. But many of them do. Nor
is all their talk lively and interesting. Sometimes, as you must
have noted, as when Christian and Hopeful, in order to keep
awake while on the Enchanted Ground, have a long discussion
that reminds us of two theological students comparing notes, the
dialogue tries our patience. Such spots, however, are over-
shadowed by the masterly dialogue that pervades the book.

Vividness of another kind brings a smile in Part II, when
one of Christiana's boys, Matthew, "gets," as Bunyan says,
"sick of the gripes." "Mr. Skill, an ancient and well approved
physician" is summoned. Like a good doctor he wants to know
what Matthew has been eating. Christiania simply can't think
what has upset her boy's stomach. But Samuel, his brother, all
too ready to tell on Matthew, speaks up. "Mother, what was that
which my brother did gather up and eat so soon as we were come
from the gate that is at the head of this way? You know that there
was an orchard on the left hand on the other side of the wall, and
some of the trees hung over the wall and my brother did pluck
and eat." Skill prescribes some symbolical pills to be taken

"three at a time, fasting, in half a quarter of a pint of the tears of repentance." There follows a delightful scene, giving us the anxious mother and the recalcitrant patient who doesn't want to take his medicine but who, when healed, is very proud of it.

Quite different is an episode when Christiana and her boys and Mercy are being conducted through the Valley of the Shadow by Greatheart. Here Bunyan shows himself a master at suggesting terror.

> Thus they went on, till they came to about the middle of the valley; and then Christiana said Methinks I see something yonder upon the road before us; a thing of such a shape as I have not seen. Then said Joseph, Mother, what is it? An ugly thing, child, an ugly thing, said she. But, Mother, what is it like? said he. 'Tis like I cannot tell what, said she. And now it is but a little way off. Then said she, It is nigh.

This is fear of the unknown set forth with an imaginative power that rivals Coleridge's grim picture in the "Ancient Mariner":

> Like one that on a lonesome road
> Doth walk in fear and dread,
> And having once turn'd round, walks on,
> And turns no more his head;
> Because he knows a frightful fiend
> Doth close behind him tread.

Interestingly enough, Coleridge once identified the secret of such suggestive power when he said: "Works of imagination should be written in a very plain language; the more purely imaginative they are the more necessary it is to be plain."

How well Bunyan does this! "I see something yonder upon the road before us; a thing of such shape as I have not seen." "What is it?" "An ugly thing, child, an ugly thing." There you have nameless dread come to life.

One of Bunyan's fine characterizations is Talkative. Christian and Faithful meet him; how Talkative lives up to his name.

He needs only to be asked a question, and the words come tumbling out. This goes on a while. Then Faithful, who is quite impressed, steps over to Christian and whispers that their new companion will make "a very excellent pilgrim." Listen to what follows:

> *Christian.* At this Christian modestly smiled, and said, This man, with whom you are so taken, will beguile with this tongue of his twenty of them that know him not.

> *Faithful.* Do you know him, then?

> *Christian.* Know him? Yes, better than he knows himself.

> *Faithful.* Pray, what is he?

> *Christian.* His name is Talkative; he dwelleth in our town. I wonder that you should be a stranger to him; only I consider that our town is large.

> *Faithful.* Whose son is he? and whereabout doth he dwell?

> *Christian.* He is the son of one Say-well; he dwelt in Prating Row; and he is known to all that are acquainted with him by the name of Talkative of Prating Row; and, notwithstanding his fine tongue, he is but a sorry fellow.

What a flair Bunyan had for names! No one, not even Dickens, ever surpassed him in putting just the right tag on his characters. Not only here but all through the book, the names capture our attention: Mr. Smooth Man, Mr. Facing Both Ways, Mr. Hold the World, Mr. Standfast, Greatheart, Mr. Valiant-for-Truth, Mrs. Timorous, Mrs. Bats Eyes, Madame Bubble. Was there ever a book with such choice names as these? And by and large they live up to their names.

But to return to Talkative, after being coached by Christian as to what to say, Faithful goes back to him. This time it's a different story. The questions probe deeper and deeper and Talkative's answers get shorter and shorter, until finally, he is off to seek other company:

> Since you are so ready to take up reports, and to judge so rashly as you do, I cannot but conclude you are some peevish and melancholic man, not fit to be discoursed with; and so adieu.

One of the nobler pieces of dialogue is in Part II at the entrance of Valiant-for-Truth, whom they meet "just at the place where Little Faith formerly was robbed." There he stands, "a man with a sword drawn, and his face all over with blood" and tells how for three hours he fought with Wild Head, Inconsiderate, and Pragmatic, whereupon Greatheart remarks:

> *Greatheart*. Then said Greatheart to Mr. Valiant-for-Truth, Thou hast worthily behaved thyself; let me see thy sword. So he showed it him. When he had taken it in his hand and looked thereon awhile, he said, Ha! it is a right Jerusalem blade.

> *Valiant-for-Truth*. It is so. Let a man have one of these blades, with a hand to wield it and skill to use it, and he might venture upon an angel with it. He need not fear its holding, if he can but tell how to lay on. Its edge will never blunt. It will cut flesh and bones, and soul and spirit, and all.

> *Greatheart*. But you fought a great while; I wonder you was not weary.

> *Valiant-for-Truth*. I fought till my sword did cleave to my hand; and then they were joined together as if a sword grew out of my arm; and when the blood ran through my fingers, then I fought with most courage.

How different from this heroic exchange is the place where Mr. Standfast talks with old Honest about meeting Madame Bubble, a lady of questionable virtue, to say the least.

Honest. Without doubt her designs were bad. But stay, now you talk with her, methinks I either have seen her, or have read some story of her.

Standfast. Perhaps you have done both.

Honest. Madame Bubble! Is she not a tall, comely dame, somewhat of a swarthy complexion?

Standfast. Right, you hit it, she is just such a one.

Honest. Doth she not speak very smoothly, and give you a smile at the end of a sentence?

Standfast. You fall right upon it again, for these are her very actions.

Honest. Doth she not wear a great purse by her side; and is not her hand often in it, fingering her money, as if that was her heart's delight?

Standfast. 'Tis just so; had she stood by all this while, you could not more amply have set her forth before me, nor have better described her features.

Standfast is right. Madame Bubble's features, and not only her features but her whole personality, could not have been better described. And with what swift precision it is done; her speaking "very smoothly" and giving "a smile at the end her speaking of a sentence," and that great purse she wears by her side with "her hand often in it, fingering her money." There she is to the very life.

Are any of you interested in writing? If you are, take a good look at *Pilgrim's Progress*. Bunyan mastered what it takes many writers a lifetime even to approach. He knew how to write simply, directly, and with complete transparency. He could do this because of the kind of man he was. If he attained to one of the very hardest of things in writing—immediacy of presentation—it was because his own experience was so intense. But he could control this intensity. Even the most vivid passages of his soul struggle in *Grace Abounding* are written with restraint.

There is nothing at all of sentimentality in Bunyan. He has great emotion but never wallows in it. Adjectives are few. Purple passages are non-existent. Action words are plentiful. He has in highest degree the power of understatement. And there's no secret about where he got these qualities. As J. R. Green said: "Bunyan's English is the simplest and homeliest English that has ever been used by any great English writer, but it is the English of the Bible. He has lived in the Bible until its words became his own."

Consider now the heart of it all. There is more to *The Pilgrim's Progress* than great art and magnificent writing. If I were to stop at this point, I should be remiss. Let me be bluntly candid. Because of the kind of person I am, and may I say, because of the kind of people I believe most of you are, Bunyan, if we will but listen to him, speaks to our condition as do few writers of any time. Moreover, I say to you that he has a particular message for young men and women in these days of turmoil and perplexity. If I learned anything through forty-one years as headmaster of a boys' college preparatory school, which meant an experience of living with young men and keeping contact with many hundreds of them as they went on to college and then into business and professional life, it is that youth abhors sham and unreality. People like you are swift to detect what is phony. They simply don't respect ersatz convictions and pretension. They have little use for those whose words don't match their lives.

Bunyan is one of the least pretentious writers the world has ever known. He had his convictions and went to jail for them. He had his soul struggle and talked about it as we don't talk about such things today. But he was real. Out of this reality he tells us some important things.

I'd like to put them as simply as possible. In these days of turmoil and perplexity, of shifting moral standards, of aimlessness and ambiguity, a lot of people seem to be confused about their identity. It's quite the thing, you know, to hear someone say, "I wonder who I really am." "What am I here for?" "What's it all about?" "What is the purpose of my life and of everything else?" "What does it all amount to?" Bunyan didn't talk like this. He didn't have our existential lingo. Yet what he says, if we get down to his rock-bottom ideas, speaks exactly to our condition today.

Don't let anybody ever tell you that while John Bunyan wrote a great book, the theological ideas of the great Puritans like him and Milton are dead and at best nothing but museum pieces in the history of thought. They are nothing of the kind. If we understand them, they are as up-to-date as the daily newspaper.

You see, Bunyan was really giving the answer to the question that lies behind all other questions, his pilgrim's question, "What must I do to be saved?" His answer isn't the least bit passé. It is relevant to those who wonder who they are and what life is all about, who are basically in a state of lostness. They haven't found themselves at the deepest level of existence.

If you ever read *Grace Abounding*, you will see that before his struggle was resolved, Bunyan labored under a terrific sense of sin. He wrestled with what psychologists today call feelings of guilt. But he won the bout in the only way anyone ever wins it—through Jesus Christ.

Now in *Pilgrim's Progress* he is honest enough to give us characters who miss out. One of the most attractive is Ignorance, a man who almost gets to the Celestial City, but is lost at the very end of the journey. The reason is that like some today, he just won't acknowledge that he is a sinner. Ignorance says, "I will never believe that my heart is thus bad." It is the same sort of attitude Van Wyck Brooks, in his *Flowering of New England*, gives us in a quotation from the mother of Charles William Eliot, the Harvard president of a former generation and a member of a Unitarian family. Brooks quotes Mrs. Eliot's remark to a friend of hers who had become an Episcopalian: "Eliza, you will never find me or any member of the Eliot family kneeling down in a church and confessing that we are miserable sinners." One of the most searching things Bunyan does for us is to face us with the inescapable fact that, if we are really to find our identity, we must recognize the break in our relationship with God because of our sin. And here he is, if you will, in accord with the best theology of our times.

Again Bunyan's intensive earnestness shows up the superficiality of present-day secularism. Everywhere there are people whose lives are empty because they have no deep commitment. They go along with the tide and seem to think that, when it comes to the great questions of the purpose of our life, our relation to the living God, our destiny, nothing more is to be expected than a middle-of-the-road, take-it-or-leave-it attitude. Bunyan didn't, as I have said, talk in our modern existential terms, but he knew the answer to the ambiguities and confusion that trouble so many of us today. Like Paul, he realized that the greatest question is not the self-centered "Who am I?" but the one Paul asked when he met the living Christ, "Who art thou, Lord?" And he learned further that more important than asking what are our plans for our lives is Paul's second question, "Lord, what wilt thou have me to do?"

It is for the daily and unavoidable responsibility for doing the truth that *Pilgrim's Progress* provides a map. As Christian said in discussing Talkative with Faithful, "The soul of religion is the practical part." Certainly no more down-to-earth book about the Christian life has ever been written than this one. In it, the Wicket Gate stands for Christ, the door to salvation, and life. But Bunyan knew very well that, if I may put modern speech into his mouth, after one enters this door, he doesn't have it completely made. There is a pilgrimage, and a fight is on. Yet the thing that sets apart Christian and Faithful and all other true pilgrims from false pilgrims like Formalist and Hypocrisy, who didn't go through the Wicket Gate but came "tumbling over the wall in the left hand of the narrow way," is that they kept on and reached their goal.

At the beginning of this essay I stressed the universality of *Pilgrim's Progress*. Few, if any, books outside the Bible have had and still have such a wide range of readers and admirers. Using the word in the very best sense, it is ecumenical. Here is a book that is the essence of Puritanism, a creed and way of life

long looked down upon by the modern mind as hopelessly narrow and out-worn. Yet it is read by children and philosophers,
great writers, believers and unbelievers, educated and unedu-
cated in almost every nation and every part of the world. Its
readership cuts across all denominational and sectarian lines.
Despite what Bunyan says about the Pope, he has had thousands
of Catholic readers.

Surely you noticed in your reading how Bunyan deals with
what the great Harvard psychologist, William James, called in
the title of his classic study of personal religion, "The Varieties
of Religious Experience." Never once does Bunyan fall into the
trap of stereotyping the way people become Christians and the
way God deals with them. In Part I, Christian's conversion was
dramatic. How different was that of Mercy, the attractive young
woman, who says to Christiana's derisive neighbors, Mrs. Bats-
eyes, Mrs. Inconsiderate, Mrs. Like-mind, and Mrs. Know-
nothing: "I think to walk this sunshiny morning a little with her
to help her on the way." In reality she has been drawn to Christiana's witness, but as Bunyan remarks, she "told . . . not of her
second reason but kept it to herself." Then when Mercy is
openly committed to go on the pilgrimage, we have this beautiful comment:

> Christiana was then glad at her heart, not only that
> she had a companion, but also for that she had pre-
> vailed with this poor maid to fall in love with her own
> salvation.

Here is a young woman who becomes a Christian simply
because she has seen that her friend has something (it would
doubtless be better to say "Someone") in her life that she does
not have and wants to have. So also with Christiana's boys, conversion is a gentle, rather than a sudden thing, and it grows out
of Christian nurture as in many a godly home. Yet it is nonetheless definite and demands a clean break with the world. Just to
compare the varieties of Christian experience in Bunyan's characters would be a study in itself. At this point, Bunyan is in accord with the deepest level of Christian psychology as expressed

so incomparably by Christ in what he said to Nicodemus: "The wind blows wherever it pleases. You hear its sound, but you cannot tell where it comes from or where it is going. So it is with everyone born of the Spirit."

It is, then, the nearness of *Pilgrim's Progress* to the spirit of Christ that gives it this universality. For a central truth that we in these days of almost endless religious discussion are liable to forget is that Christ transcends all churches and all denominations. He is not a sectarian figure. He came as the Savior of all men who will come to him in the way set forth in Scripture.

Yes, *Pilgrim's Progress* is a map to the Christian life. But if it is such, it is first of all because the book is throughout so biblical. In the fascination of the various characters Bunyan so vitally portrays, we must never forget the enduring significance of the roll he carries with him. That roll represents the Bible. When he loses it or forgets it, Pilgrim goes astray. If his journey and that of his companions and if the journey of Christiana and her companions provide us with a roadmap to Christian living, it is because they walked according to the Book of books. How well Bunyan knew what many of us are too lazy to follow through with—that it is impossible really to live the Christian life apart from the Bible and its instruction.

Let me say as plainly as possible that you will have missed the best *Pilgrim's Progress* can give you if you do not see its indissoluble relation to the Bible. If the spirit of *Pilgrim's Progress* grips you, you will be inevitably drawn closer to the one book without which it would have been impossible for Bunyan to have written what he did and as he did.

Perhaps since you received your assignment to study *Pilgrim's Progress*, you have been asking the question, "Why?" "Why read something as old and quaint as this, and why keep on reading it?" There are good literary and cultural answers to these questions, but more important is another answer. It takes us back to the title of this essay, "Encounter with Greatness." I give it to you now in the words of one of the really great modern philosophers, Alfred North Whitehead. "Moral education is impossible apart from the habitual vision of greatness." This is what Bunyan shows us in the *Pilgrim's Progress*, nothing less than an authentic vision of greatness. Indeed, it is a vision not just of greatness, but of the greatest of all.

And observe that Whitehead speaks of "the habitual vision." The inference is plain. It's not enough to take a single look at great literature. We must keep on looking at it. One reading, two readings won't do. You all face a test quite apart from the quizzes and examinations your teachers give you. It is this. Will you read *Pilgrim's Progress* again? Will you keep on reading it, as some of us keep on reading it? That leads me to a challenge. By all means read and read again the *Pilgrim's Progress*. But even this is not enough. The only way really to know Bunyan is with your Bible in your hand. For were he here he would tell us that everything he was and did was from God through the written Word and through the incarnate Word, Jesus Christ, to whom his book bears such enduring witness. For the true life-giving encounter with greatness is that of the individual with Jesus Christ, to whom Bunyan and his book and the Bible so clearly point. Have you encountered him?

PART 5

LEISURE

The Christian Use of Leisure

W ith the five-day work week, most Americans enjoy an amount of free time unknown to former generations. While the number of hours worked during the year fell rapidly between 1940 and 1960, the decline, although slowed since the advent of the forty-hour week, continues. But working less and less for more and more leisure is not making us a happier or a better people. Leisure time is a potential rather than an inherent good. Its beneficial employment demands the exercise of personal responsibility, for few things are so demoralizing as the abuse of leisure. What we do with our free time is a matter of Christian concern.

Underneath the misuse of leisure is the lack of those inner resources that make possible the right use of solitude. As Pascal put it in a flash of insight, "All the unhappiness of men arises from one single fact, that they cannot stay quietly in their own chamber."[1]

The emptiness of soul that makes solitude unbearable for so many leads to the restless search that so marks our times—the search for satisfaction through new and more exciting ways of being entertained. The shared pleasures of the group are not necessarily inferior; man is a social being, and his nature requires fellowship. But what he brings to this fellowship reflects what he is within himself. And still the paradox remains that those who are best able to entertain themselves through good reading, music, art, the personal enjoyment of nature, and other worthy avocations derive most from group recreation.

Christians today live in a state of tension with the world and its culture. Nowhere is this tension more acute than in the realm of leisure. The answer to the problem is not to list the multitudinous varieties of leisure-time pursuits, and then to declare some good and some bad. That way lies legalism. Obviously there are in the light of the Word of God things that are clearly wrong and others that are clearly right. The difficulty resides in the ambiguities about which committed Christians disagree.

Moreover, the binding obligation of witnessing for Christ cannot be discharged in a social vacuum. To ask, as did Tertullian, "What has Athens to do with Jerusalem?" and then to retreat into cultural isolationism will not do for us today. Christians must know the culture that surrounds them if they are to make their witness understood. But there is a difference between knowledge of or about something and identification with it. Our culture contains elements the defiling nature of which we know full well and in which we participate at our soul's peril.

Here is the real point of tension respecting the Christian use of leisure. As Milton says in a great sentence in his *Areopagitica*, "I cannot praise a fugitive and cloistered virtue, unexercised and unbreathed, that never sallies out and sees her adversary, but slinks out of the race, where that immortal garland is to be run for, not without dust and heat." So the Christian in an unchristian culture must have the fortitude, as Milton says in the same context, to "see and know and yet abstain."

The Reformation doctrine of the inner witness of the Holy Spirit reaches beyond its application to the Scriptures. For those who are Christ's in a spiritually alien culture, it provides the essential safeguard in the inevitable encounter with the world in which they live and to which they are obligated to communicate the gospel. The Spirit who indwells every Christian can be trusted to show the believer who knows his Bible where in his obligatory contacts with the culture of his time he must draw the line.

In an exhaustive study of the problem of leisure in British life (*English Life and Leisure*, by R. Seebohm Rowntree and G. R. Lavers), religion is treated along with the cinema, the stage, broadcasting, dancing, and reading, as a leisure-time pursuit. This strange misconception of the role of religion in life is all too common even among church members. Whether a Christian uses his leisure for playing a musical instrument, painting pictures, reading adventure stories, gardening, mountain climbing, bowling, or any one of a thousand other things, is an optional matter. God has given us a host of pursuits richly to enjoy. The scriptural criterion of what we may do is unequivocally stated by Paul in Colossians 3:17, "And whatever you do, whether in word or deed, do it all in the name of the Lord Jesus, giving thanks to God the Father through him." But religion (using the word in the high sense of the practice of Christianity) is not for the believer an elective, spare-time pursuit like going to football games or bird-watching. It is life itself, and it comprehends everything Christians do and say and hear and think. To be sure, certain practices of religion, such as attendance at church, reading the Bible, visiting the sick, and helping the underprivileged, are done in time apart from the daily job. Yet the claims of Jesus Christ are all-inclusive. Nothing is ever irrelevant to him with whom we have to do.

Christ is the Lord of time—of free time as well as of working time. Those who are his are responsible for the stewardship of the time he gives them. One of the great New Testament phrases is the twice-repeated one of the Apostle, "redeeming the time" (Ephesians 5:16; Colossians 4:5, KJV). Our Lord himself lived under the pressing stewardship of time, as we know from his reiterated "my time has not yet come."

How Christians use their time in a time-wasting world is crucial to their spiritual outreach. "Eternity—for some who can't spend one half hour profitably!" President Eliot of Harvard once exclaimed. God entrusts us with nothing more valuable than time. Without it money is valueless and the stewardship of money meaningless. Literature has few more pathetic passages than the vain plea for time at the end of Marlowe's *Faustus*:

> Stand still, you ever-moving spheres of heaven,
> That time may cease, and midnight never come;
> Fair Nature's eye, rise, rise again, and make
> Perpetual day; or let this hour be but
> A year, a month, a week, a natural day
> That Faustus may repent and save his soul!

The very word *leisure* implies responsibility. Central to its dictionary meaning is the idea of freedom afforded by nonworking time. But in Christian life and practice freedom is always conditioned by responsibility. Our liberty is to be used to the glory of God. We are accountable for the stewardship of our leisure as well as of our working time. From the daily occupation there is indeed leisure, but from the unremitting exercise of Christian responsibility there is no such thing as spare time. No Christian is ever off-duty for God. Leisure and working time are equally to be accounted for to the Lord who said, "Open your eyes and look at the fields! They are ripe for harvest" (John 4:35).

"The Christian Use of Leisure," Notes

1. *Pensees*, II, 139.

Mountain Views

*N*o mountaineer of any experience can long escape being asked, "Why do you climb?" Now there may be behind that question more than idle curiosity. There may be behind it an attitude toward mountains, carried over unconsciously from the Middle Ages. Not until the end of the eighteenth century did men look at the jagged rocks and perpetual snows of the high mountains as anything but terrifying excrescences upon the face of nature. Only through firsthand knowledge, gained by exploring the glaciers and climbing the rocky heights, did fear give way to appreciation of the beauty of the great ranges. Or, if modern men have lost this fear of the mountains, they may see little use in climbing their summits. The hazards seem too great and the exercise too strenuous for most people to take the trouble of climbing nowadays.

But the view of mountains reflected in the Bible is different from the superstitious awe of the Middle Ages or the lazy unconcern of many today. In contrast to the general avoidance of mountains in medieval times, there are in Scripture, even more than in other ancient literature, many references to them, far outnumbering references to the other leading aspect of nature, the sea. From the mention in Genesis 8:4 of Ararat, the great 17,000-foot peak in Armenia, capped by its glittering ice dome, to Revelation 21:10, where John in his vision is transported to a high mountain, whence he sees the New Jerusalem in all her splendor, the Word of God is full of mountains. Names like Ararat, Moriah, Sinai, Horeb, Zion, Carmel, Hermon, Gerizim, Olivet, and Calvary have rich associations; indeed the basic structure of sacred history might be related to the mountains of Scripture. And in respect to poetry, some of the most sublime imagery in the Old Testament has to do with mountains.

But most appealing to the Christian is the place mountains occupy in the life and ministry of the Lord Jesus. To them he withdrew for solitary prayer. From a lofty summit the devil showed him all the kingdoms of this world. Two of his greatest sermons were spoken in the hills. It may well have been on the flanks of Hermon, the dominant peak of Lebanon, that he was transfigured and his garments shone white as the snows. Nor can we ever forget that "the cross on which the Prince of Glory died" was set upon a hill.

Despite this wealth of sacred association, the attitude toward mountains in Scripture differs from our feeling today. Climbing as we know it was not done in Bible times. As has already been stated, for the first seventeen hundred years of the Christian Era there was little attempt to explore the great mountain ranges. Exceptions there were, of course, such as the Emperor Hadrian's climb of Etna in Sicily; the venturesome Leonardo da Vinci, who explored part of the Monte Rosa range; and the soldiers of Cortez who in 1519 struggled up the icy cone of Popocatepetl in Mexico to get sulfur. But it was the ascent of Mont Blanc by Balmat in 1786 that began the mountaineering of our times. Following this conquest of the topmost point of Western Europe, the British took up climbing, and in the nineteenth century first developed it as a recreation. Great Alpine summits were ascended by men like Tyndale, Leslie Stephen, Mummery, Whymper, and their Swiss and French guides.

"But what," the nonclimber asks, "has all this to do with my question? Why," he persists, "do you climb?" The answer is that climbing mountains reflects an attitude toward them. We who find our recreation in the high hills do so because we love them. George Leigh Mallory, who with his young companion Irvine disappeared in 1924 within a thousand feet of the summit of Mt. Everest, spoke for every mountaineer when he answered the question as to why he wanted to climb Everest by simply saying, "Because it's there."

Only the tiny minority of climbers will ever see, let alone attempt, the great Himalayan summits; yet when we look up at Mt. Hood or Rainier, the Grand Teton or the Matterhorn, or even Mt. Washington or Katahdin, we also feel as Mallory did of Everest. Between us and the great hills there is a pull, not easy of definition, but none the less real. The mountain before which we stand is a challenge; our eyes measure its difficulties, and we want to test out its cliffs and couloirs, its snowfields and glaciers. But the nonclimber is different. He may delight in the beauty of a mountain, but he admires it from afar.

In my own case, several mountains were the magnets that drew me to climbing. The first was Pike's Peak in the Rockies. The sight of its huge, reddish bulk looming beyond Colorado Springs stirred the urge to climb it, and a small boy's persistence (I was eleven at the time) was rewarded by the nine-mile trudge up the cog railway with my mining engineer brother. Another mountain that helped make me a climber was Mt. Hood in the Cascades. The transcontinental train had stopped along the Columbia River, and there, piercing the blue air above the dark green forests, was the north face of Hood, a glorious pyramid clad in shining snow. For a boy of sixteen it was an unforgettable vision of mountain beauty and a challenge fulfilled by two ascents of this peak many years later. Influential also were the gentler summits of the Catskills, beloved by my father, with whom I walked many miles in those beautifully wooded and historic mountains of New York State. For he too was a lover of the hills, though not a climber in the technical sense.

Yes, we climb in response to a challenge. And the challenge has many facets. Not only is it a response to beauty; it has also in it the lure of the difficult. Modern life is a strange mixture of tension and luxury. While nerves are taxed by the hurry and competition of our towns and cities, physically we are becoming flabby. Very few Americans know how to walk. Where our parents would have walked—to church, to the store, round the block to visit a friend—we ride in cars. Mountaineering is a challenge because it demands physical hardship. No one ever climbs a great peak without getting up early, usually before sunrise, without eating sparingly of simple food, without going on when he is very tired, without exposure to burning sun or icy wind, and without at times overcoming fear.

These things are not easy; they spell discipline of hand and foot and emotion. But they are good in a time when the combination of nervous strain and physical softness is all too common, even among Christians. The bow that is always tightly strung loses the resiliency; and even the strongest constitution must relax. Our Lord voiced an abiding principle of the Christian life when he said to his disciples, "Come with me by yourselves to a quiet place [quite possibly the Galilean hills] and get some rest." To be sure, mountaineering is but one of many forms of outdoor recreation, yet those of us who follow it thank God for the refreshment it brings.

Climbing, then, has its rewards, and they are not all physical. There is truth in the lines of that mystical poet, William Blake:

> Great things are done when men and mountains
>   meet:
> These are not done by scurrying in the street.

Everyone who has climbed at all extensively knows something of Blake's meaning, though he may find it hard to put into words. I think, for example, of a sunny midday on the summit rocks of the Middle Teton in Wyoming. It was 1942. Preaching appointments had taken me to the Far West, and there was opportunity for some climbing. It was a memorable day from the four-o'clock start; trudging up the trail in the dark, seeing the dawn over Jackson Hole, walking in the early morning sun on the snow that filled upper Garnet Canyon early that July, climbing on crampons the frozen couloir to the col between the South and Middle Tetons, breasting the wind as it came rushing across the col from the Idaho side of the range, and finally looking for holds up the steep rocks to the summit. And the reward was just to sit there astride a sun-warmed granite block, nearly thirteen thousand feet above sea level, gazing down six thousand feet on Jenny Lake, with the few buildings like toy houses, and looking up at the tremendous obelisk of the Grand Teton, soaring dramatically into the almost indigo sky. It was quiet with the utter stillness of the high solitudes. The sun shone brightly. And the stillness brought with it a deep, inner peace. Prayer and grateful rededication to the Lord who created such grandeur came almost unbidden from my heart. The long descent was made with spirit refreshed by an experience the memory of which abides as a permanent and treasured possession.

Another of the intangible rewards of climbing is the renewed sense of perspective. We go to the mountains with our problems—personal, business, or professional. And somehow, as we consider them on some friendly summit or under the heavens with the stars shining so brightly through the thin air, they do not loom large. We see them more clearly and in their proper place. At other times we may be too busy looking for the next hand or foothold or belaying our companion to think of them specifically, yet the mind and eye that become used to the heights and depths and spacious vistas of the mountains learn to evaluate the daily problems from the perspective of truth rather than the distortion of worry.

Not the least among the rewards of climbing is a memory stored with pictures that those remaining in the valleys never see. Surely one of the results of an active love for mountains is the enrichment of what Augustine in his *Confessions* called "the fields and spacious palaces" of memory. To the lover of the high places of God's creation, there is continuing joy in the remembrance of beauty experienced in personal encounter with the hills. A mountain climbed, especially if the ascent has taxed strength and skill, is a mountain that has become personalized for the climber. Memories of its individuality and structure, recollections of storm and sunshine, views awesome and friendly, heartwarming remembrance of goodly fellowship in tent, at the campfire, and on the rope—these become part of the mental furnishing of those who find recreation in the mountains. Whoever comes to climbing with receptive heart and seeing eye will find much that, being true and pure, lovely and of good report, belongs in the charter of Christian thought set forth in the last chapter of Philippians.

William Blake is right: "Great things are done when men and mountains meet." The climber may find it hard to put all these things into words for others to understand. But he knows that the intangible compensations of climbing can never be "gained by scurrying in the street." They come through strenuous exertion, through the discipline of mastery over self, and, in their highest expression, through renewal of the faith that sees in the God of creation one so great that he "weighed the mountains on the scales and the hills in a balance," yet so gracious that he gave his Son, through whom all things were made, for the redemption of us men.

PART 6

CHRISTIAN HUMANISM

Evangelicals and
Social Concern[1]

*E*vangelical social concern is no new thing. Nearly eighty years ago the church historian, F. J. Foakes-Jackson, wrote:

> No branch indeed of the Western Church can be refused the honor of having assisted in the progress of humane ideas and non-Christians have participated largely in the work of diffusing the modern spirit of kindness; but the credit for the inception of the movement belongs without doubt to that form of Protestantism which is distinguished by the importance it attaches to the doctrine of the Atonement. . . . History shows that the thought of Christ on the cross has been more potent than anything else in arousing compassion for suffering and indignation at injustice. . . . The later Evangelicalism, which saw in the death of Christ the means of free salvation for fallen humanity, caused its adherents to take the front rank as champions of the weak. . . . Prison reform, the prohibition of the slave trade, the abolition of

slavery, the Factory Acts, the protection of children, the crusade against cruelty to animals, are all the outcome of the Great Evangelical Revival of the eighteenth century. The humanitarian tendencies of the nineteenth century, which it is but just to admit all Christian communities have fostered, and which non-Christian philanthropists have vied with them in encouraging, are among the greatest triumphs of the power and influence of Christ.

Yes, the record is clear. Such classic studies as Timothy Smith's *Revivalism and Social Reform* and, in relation to the effects of the Wesleyan revival, J. W. Bready's *England: Before and After Wesley* document our heritage in social involvement.

But toward the end of the last century and in the early years of the present one, along with the rise of the social gospel and the emergence of modernism in America, something happened to social concern among fundamentalists. (I use the word because our current usage of *evangelical* and *conservative evangelical* arose later). Fundamentalist social concern went into an eclipse. This was due in great part to that earlier "battle for the Bible" in which fundamentalist leaders closed their ranks against modernism with its denial of basic Christian doctrine and its link with the more radical biblical criticism. Also, in their zeal for defending the gospel and the Scriptures, these leaders reacted against the social gospel being promoted by the liberal Protestant establishment.

The term *social gospel* (surely unfortunate in view of Galatians 1:6-9) stems from the name of a magazine published by members of the Georgia Commonwealth Colony, a Christian communistic group that resided from 1895 to 1900 on a thousand-acre tract in the state of Georgia. The term was picked up in 1905 by Shailer Mathews and others and became "the accepted name for social Christianity."

From its beginning, the social gospel was linked to evolution and socialism. It stressed social salvation at the expense of individual salvation. So it was not surprising that the fundamentalists opposed it. Moreover their preoccupation with predictive prophecy, especially as the First World War came, contributed to the eclipse of social concern among them. That the two groups—fundamentalist and modernist, the one promoting personal evangelism and the other the social gospel—were thoroughly polarized is evident. For example, C. H. Hopkins's definitive study, *The Rise of the Social Gospel in American Protestantism*, makes no mention whatever of D. L. Moody, R. A. Torrey, Billy Sunday, or even of Robert E. Speer.

Sherwood Wirt has summed up the situation like this:

> The weakness of the Bible defender of the recent past was not so much his premises or his logic, as his failure to look out for the needs of his neighbors. He was too often blinded by the smoke of the theological brushfires and unable to see what was happening to his world. The social conscience of the evangelical went into rigor mortis.

But rigor mortis follows death, and social conscience did not die, as Wirt himself went on to show. It rather became, in Carl F. H. Henry's phrase, an "uneasy conscience." Even at the most drastic point of its eclipse, evangelical social concern continued through such efforts as rescue missions, prison visitation, opposition to the liquor traffic, and once-removed social work on the foreign mission field. And despite the regrettable slowness of the evangelical community by and large in responding to issues that were coming to the fore in the fifties and sixties—issues like civil rights, political and religious persecution and torture, hunger and poverty, and the nuclear threat—today there are signs of what may well be a renaissance of social concern among evangelicals. For the first time various segments of evangelicalism, ranging from the politically radical through the politically liberal and centrist to the politically rightist and far right, are speaking out. Names come readily to mind: Sojourners, *The Other Side*, Voice of Calvary, Evangelicals for Social Action Commission, National Black Evangelical Association,

World Vision, Prison Fellowship, Moral Majority. Nor should we overlook the social agencies of the evangelical denominations themselves.

Amid this diversity a significant trend is, I think, developing: On certain issues like hunger (witness the broad consensus in Bread for the World), abortion (on which *Sojourners Magazine* has taken a conservative stand) and pornography (to which *The Other Side* devoted an issue), evangelicals on both the left and the right have to some extent been at one in voicing their convictions. And the same trend is now developing in the concern about the build-up of nuclear armaments.

So far I have been writing descriptively and by way of background. Let us turn now to some biblical principles that must underlie a truly evangelical social concern. Doing this will require us to face some of the shortcomings and unfinished business of our social concern and reassess certain attitudes that can blunt it. Above all, it will entail bringing our social efforts under the criticism of the Word of God both written and incarnate.

Here, then, are two assumptions that have restricted and in some circles continue to restrict the full exercise of the neighbor love to which Christ obligates us. Both need reexamination in the light of Scripture.

The first may be stated like this: *Just preach the gospel so that people are born again and then changed people will bring about the needed social change*. But this rests on a simplistic view of evangelism. It mixes the truth that Christian social action has come and can come from people changed by Christ—it mixes this with a truncated view of our Lord's Great Commission. For Matthew 28:19-20 combines evangelism ("go and make disciples of all nations, baptizing them") with obedience to all Christ taught ("teaching them to obey everything I have commanded you"). At the heart of Christ's teaching is loving concern for others. Just as clearly as the New Testament tells us that salvation is only by grace through faith and in no way by works, so it binds us in total discipleship to the ministry of compassion to which we have been saved. Unmistakably the New

Testament links Christ's giving himself for us with our giving ourselves for others.

> This how we know what love is: Jesus Christ laid down his life for us. And we ought to lay down our lives for our brothers. If anyone has material possessions and sees his brother in need but has no pity on him, how can the love of God be in him? (1 John 3:16-17).

Neither Christ nor the New Testament writers spoke of a kind of disembodied salvation. As Albert Schweitzer said, in Jesus' parable of the lost sheep it was the whole sheep that was saved. The failure to link the essential preaching about being born again with the obligation to obey all of Christ's commands is the reason why in some places where the altar call has been most insistently given certain great social injustices were tolerated so long.

A second assumption that has restricted evangelical social concern asserts this: *A conservative evangelical theology necessarily means a conservative social outlook.* But this too is unbiblical. For one thing it reflects a misunderstanding of the basic nature of biblical prophecy, which includes far more than its eschatological element on which some evangelicals have concentrated almost to the exclusion of listening to the burning words of the prophets about the poor, about oppression and injustice, about wealth gained through the exploitation, idolatry, and disobedience to God's righteous requirements, and about the hollowness of worship by people who are blind and deaf to human need.

The other day I completed an extended study of the book of Amos at a weekly Bible study breakfast in Washington that I have been leading for about fifteen years. The group—professional men mostly of politically conservative outlook—needed little prompting from me to see the application of Amos to our society right now.

And Amos does not stand alone. The strain of godly social

concern runs throughout all the prophets, major as well as minor, and indeed throughout the entire Old Testament. In *Christianity Today* (2 October 1981) I spoke about the unbalanced, over-selective use of Scripture into which we evangelicals are prone to slip. It is a strange paradox, is it not? The very people who affirm with all their hearts the inerrancy of the whole Bible seem content to overlook great sections of its most probing teaching.

It is not only our comparative neglect of the Old Testament that has contributed to our lag in social concern but also our restricted use of the New Testament. Take, for example, the neglect of our Lord's teaching about the kingdom. Back in 1947 Carl F. H. Henry said, "There is a growing reluctance to explicate the kingdom idea in fundamentalist preaching"—to which I would add that this reluctance still persists in much evangelical preaching today. What right have we to evade the subject to which our Lord devoted the major portion of his teaching, including some of his most searching words? Is neglect of the teaching about the kingdom in the synoptics—it is mentioned fifty-five times in Matthew, twenty times in Mark, forty-six times in Luke, but only five times in John—is this one reason for imbalance in evangelical preaching? Can it be that some of us are not sure about how to cope with the great kingdom passages like the Sermon on the Mount? Be that as it may, preaching and teaching that slides over the more drastic words of Jesus in the synoptics—and many of us have done this—is bound to be deficient in biblical social concern.

No, a conservative theology, if we mean by that a theology that takes the whole of Scripture seriously, does not necessarily demand a conservative social outlook.

Let me turn now to a basic criterion for evangelical social concern. Because we are evangelicals, such a criterion must be both biblical and Christ-centered. I believe that in our Lord's Good Shepherd allegory in John 10, we have a definitive criterion for our social concern. These are the words: "I have come that they may have life, and have it to the full" (v. 10). It was for this purpose that our Lord Jesus Christ was incarnate, that he lived and taught and ministered to human need, that he died and rose again. The gospel is preeminently related to life at its highest and fullest—life in its eternal dimension and also life here and now. Hence anything that denies, threatens, mars, or diminishes human life must be the object of our active Christian concern. A criterion like this one sanctions the whole spectrum of our Christian social concern. Under it come the great life issues like hunger, abortion, persecution and torture, racism, violence (including that on the highways), pornography, alcoholism and drug abuse, and nuclear war. All these—and others too—are related to life and to having it to the full.

In view of this criterion, are there any areas of concern where evangelicals have unfinished business? Obviously those in which we are already active come under that classification because they are still ongoing concerns. But there are other areas where our evangelical social concern has been, I think, much too minimal. Let me point out only three of them.

The first, *the environmental issue*, relates to the quality of human life here and now and in the future. Its biblical roots go back to the cultural mandate in Genesis and to the principle of stewardship. God placed man in the garden (the archetypal symbol of our environment) not to despoil it but to work it and care for it. We do not really own any of it. The environment is entrusted to us—the lands, the waters, the atmosphere, plant and animal life—to use for human sustenance and betterment, not to squander for immediate gain and this at the risk of threatening the life of future generations. Nuclear war threatens sudden obliteration of human life. Persistent despoiling of the environment threatens gradual but ultimate destruction of human life. Thus far those who have been most concerned about the environment have not been notable for their biblical and Christian motivation. Yet the issue persists, and evangelicals must put it higher on their agenda.

Another piece of unfinished business relates to *the place of women* in our society. Evangelicals were divided on the Equal Rights Amendment. But there are areas, quite apart from constitutional action, in which women need greater freedom and more support and recognition. An attitude of male domination rather than of mutual submission in Christ still persists among us and we need to do more about it.

One more issue in which evangelicals need to become far more involved is that of *nuclear war*. To be sure, some evangelical leaders have already taken a stand on this matter—for example, those who in 1976 signed "A Call to Faithfulness," a manifesto against nuclear armaments. Since then, concern about this paramount subject has been growing among us. Still the redundant build-up of nuclear armaments seems to evoke very little concern among the rank and file of evangelicals. Rather does passive and uncritical acceptance continue to be the attitude of a great many of us. Some evangelicals have been saying that God will not allow mankind to destroy itself through nuclear holocaust. If this is really their conviction, then outspoken opposition to the build-up of nuclear weapons at a cost that is crippling essential social programs would seem incumbent on them. One other thought: If anything like the kind of intense concern many evangelicals bring to issues such as prolife, pornography, and prayer in the public schools were to be devoted to an evangelical protest against the proliferation of nuclear arms, a courageous stand for life would be made in the name of the Prince of Peace and the race toward destruction might be slowed.

Like all godly endeavor, evangelical social concern does not go unopposed. As Paul said to Timothy, "Everyone who wants to live a godly life in Christ Jesus will be persecuted." It is doubtful whether any Christian life devoid of social concern can really be a godly one. Opposition to godly and concerned living has many forms, including most of all the unremitting pressures of the greedy materialism that pervades our culture and even seeps into Christian homes and churches.

Some of my readers have childhood memories of the Great Depression that struck our country in the early thirties. Many of you were not yet born when it happened. I am one who had to cope with it as an adult—in my case, as head of a school. And this I can tell you. There is a vast difference between the mood in which people faced the hard times fifty years ago—times far, far harder than ours—and the way people are facing economic problems today. In an article in the *Los Angeles Times* (1981) based on a study of personal letters from ordinary people in the Great Depression, Robert S. McElvaine of Millsaps College calls the people of the thirties the "us" generation because of their willingness to work and make sacrifices together, whereas today we have, he says, the "me" generation in which an insidious spirit of selfishness characterizes a society so accustomed to affluence that it will not let it go. From personal experience I can assure you that McElvaine's conclusions are correct.

This too I know. The prevalent confusion of success with material things and the growing sense of entitlement to more and more possessions—and evangelicals are by no means free from it— can cut the nerve of compassionate concern for our suffering brothers and sisters for whom Christ died.

Observe again the words of the apostle John: "Jesus Christ laid down his life for us. And we ought to lay down our lives for our brothers." Here is the ultimate dynamic for evangelical social concern. But what is it to lay down your life for your brother or sister? Does John mean only the ultimate act of heroism? I think not. I think that laying down one's life for others can and should be a repeated action. It means caring more about people than dollars and things. It means taking part of the life span the Lord allots us and laying it down for our neighbors.

The *Denver Post* (December 1981) told of a twelve-year-old girl, both legally blind and mentally retarded, who is an inmate of the Colorado State Home for the retarded and multiply handicapped. With just a glimmer of sight she could cast her eyes upward to the lights on a Christmas tree. "She has no parents; no one ever comes to see her," the therapist said. It is a situation that can be duplicated thousands of times in similar institutions all over the country. Yet how few care enough even to lay down one hour of their lives to show others who are in need (and they are not just in institutions but all around us) a reflection of the love Christ has lavished on us.

We can and must give our money to causes that demand

our evangelical social concern. But not even the most generous gifts can take the place of laying down our lives through giving some of our time, our very lives, to the personal practice of Christian social concern.

Years ago a missionary in North Africa wrote these familiar words:

> Turn your eyes upon Jesus.
> Look full in His wonderful face,
> And the things of earth
> Will grow strangely dim
> In the light of His glory and grace.

A beloved expression of pietism, yet open, I think, to some questions. Yes, at the heart of Christianity and at the heart of our concern there must be the vision of Christ. But the face of Christ to which we turn our eyes in fullest devotion is not the one portrayed in the sentimental pictures of him we put on the walls of our homes and Sunday schools. No, it is the face of the Christ who laid down his life for us, the face of the Christ on the cross, the face that was marred more than that of any man. We look at him and see the crown of thorns and his atoning blood. And when we see him in this way, the needs of this lost word become not "strangely dim" but terribly and compellingly real. For if our hearts are open to him in obedient discipleship, we hear him saying to us what he said to the first believers: " 'As the Father has sent me, I am sending you' " (John 20:21).

"Evangelicals and Social Concern," Notes

1. This essay originally appeared in the *Journal of the Evangelical Theological Society* 25, no. 1 (March 1982), 17ff., and is used by permission.

The Humanities and the Vision of Greatness: The Case for a Contemporary Christian Humanism

*T*he Renaissance opened the eyes of Europe "to the glory that was Greece/and the grandeur that was Rome." Though largely secular, it was by no means wholly so. Many of the humanists like Erasmus and Colet were Christians. Luther, Melanchthon, Calvin, and other reformers were classically trained scholars, and there was a living relationship between the intellectual flowering of the Renaissance and the spiritual rebirth of the Reformation. It's well to remember this in view of the not inconsiderable number in Protestant churches who consider the humanities a sort of fringe on the garment of education. As Professor Yaroslav Pelikan has remarked, "The Protestant Reformation was launched by a cadre of intellectuals, but the latterday heirs of the Reformation sometimes seem determined to do everything they can to live it down."

Since the Renaissance, the humanities have, of course, embraced much more than the Latin and Greek classics. Nor is there precise agreement on what should be included in them. To be sure, everyone places English and its literature, the other languages and their literatures, and the arts and philosophy among them. But there the consensus stops. Some put religion and theology with the humanities, others do not. And what about history? Many include it under the social sciences. But is history a science or an art? And is it on its higher levels literature, and so among the humanities, as it was in the past? Moreover, mathematics with its profound philosophical aspects has had its place among the humanities.

But regardless of how narrow or broad its definition, the idea of the humanities is a unitive one. Actually, none of the individual disciplines stands in isolation from the others; each is an indispensable strand in "the web of knowledge." There is a wholeness in learning we must be careful not to break. Schism is a sin, not just spiritually but also intellectually. "You must not," said Alfred North Whitehead, "divide the seamless coat of learning." The humanities are part of a total landscape of reality, and whatever of truth we find in them does not stand alone. If God is, as Isaiah declared, "The God of truth," then all truth is his—whether in philosophy or science, literature or mathematics.

Now what is it that sets the humanities apart from the other disciplines? Essentially it is their relationship to what makes us human, to that which gives us our unique dignity—namely, the *imago Dei* within us. They show us that we who are made in the image of the Creator can be creative in our human way. We call literature, philosophy, and the arts *humanities* because they are so distinctively human. What animal ever engaged in abstract philosophical thinking? (One asks the question confidently, despite the amusing little passage in the *Republic*, where Socrates speaks of the dog as a philosopher.) Or what animal ever consciously made art? Why, as G. K. Chesterton said, "Art is the signature of man," a statement that applies to other of the humanities as well.

Think of the uniqueness of language and writing. Consider the glory of the word, so human yet so divine, because God used human language to reveal his truth to us and because his Son spoke in plain, everyday words with a power and beauty that have never been surpassed. Think too of how in the humanities we see man in the totality of his nature—at the height of his glory and in the depth of his fall. As Paul Tillich has pointed out, literature and the arts mirror what man really is. Moreover, they serve not only as the vehicle of truth but also of falsehood.

In the preface to her novel, *Horizon*, Helen McInnes says:

> False pretenses in the world of ideas . . . can be as deadly in their effect as the adulteration of food. The writer who alters the facts of history, or twists events into a false pattern, to suit his own ideas, is providing his readers with his own package of particular poison. The mind is more vulnerable than the stomach, because it can be poisoned without feeling immediate pain.

A lie in science or economics can have drastic consequences physically or materially. But a lie in art or literature or philosophy can have eternal consequences.

"What is man that you are mindful of him?" That question from the Eighth Psalm must be faced in any consideration of the humanities. Yes, what is man, the only creature with the capability of making works of literature and art and constructing philosophies that probe the meaning of life? Despite its easy dismissal by many in this secular age, the biblical view of man's origin and worth is not obsolete. Every educated person should know what Scripture says "Of man's first disobedience, and the fruit of the forbidden tree/whose mortal taste brought death into the world." To go to Genesis and confront the archetypal source material, so influential in human life and culture, should dispel many of the misconceptions of the biblically illiterate among the intellectuals.

Nor can one know who man is in the sense that underlies the Renaissance and Reformation unless he is acquainted at firsthand with the primary sources of Pauline and Augustinian theology. What does that universal generalization, "all have sinned and fall short of the glory of God" (Romans 3:23) mean? Can we save ourselves; or, to put it in current jargon, can we extricate ourselves from our own existential dilemma? Do we need the grace of God in Christ to bring us to a personal renaissance? These are no casual questions; they go to the heart of our human situation today as in the past. The answers to them in classical theology stemming from Scripture, as all Christian theology ultimately does, have been so influential in literature, art, music, philosophy—indeed, the entire gamut of culture—that they demand more than the sketchy impressions so many otherwise educated people have of them.

Now to say, as some Christians have done, that because man is a fallen creature he is therefore in himself essentially nothing, is to distort both Scripture and theology. Man, who is made in the image of God, is not a cipher. Few biblical doctrines have been so misunderstood as that of human depravity. It does not mean that man is worthless in God's sight, nor does it mean that the fall wiped out the *imago Dei*. On the contrary, Scripture stresses the redeemability of man and tells what God did to reconcile the world to himself. Though the image of God was irretrievably marred, it was not destroyed; for through common grace man can be wonderfully creative. That is the biblical view of man. And it is at the heart of Christian humanism, which is not an anachronism but as valid an option today as it was for an Erasmus, a Melanchthon, or a Pascal, and in our times for a Jacques Maritain or a C. S. Lewis.

At this point, mention must be made of another view—that of secular humanism, a position that goes back to the Renaissance and that many hold to now. It makes man himself a kind of creator in his own right and gives him sole credit for his achievement. But let us leave it for the moment, as we turn to "the vision of greatness."

The words come from Alfred North Whitehead's famous sentence in his *Aims of Education*: "Moral education is impossible apart from the habitual vision of greatness." In itself it's a great statement and merits Sir Richard Livingstone's comment, "Outside Plato, there is no profounder saying about education." Yet like every other memorable saying it must be seen in its context, which is Whitehead's chapter on "The Place of the Classics in Education." He wanted Latin literature right at the center, because it tells about ancient Rome and its leaders and civilization.

> The merit of this study in the education of youth, is
> its concreteness, its inspiration to action, and the uni-
> form greatness of persons in their characters and
> their staging. Their aims were great, their virtues
> were great, and their vices were great. They had the
> saving merit of sinning with cart-ropes. Moral educa-
> tion is impossible apart from the habitual vision of
> greatness. If we are not great, it does not matter what
> we do or what is the issue.

Well, Whitehead was a distinguished philosopher, and *The Aims
of Education* is an important book. Nevertheless we must look
critically at what he said.

This oft-quoted phrase, "the vision of greatness" or, to be
precise, "the habitual vision of greatness," epitomizes the central issue of education not only in the humanities but in every
other field of learning. Moreover, it's an issue that applies to all
of life and the whole of knowledge. For it leads to the question
of perspective or world view. In what context do we look at
learning and life—not sometimes but always, not now and then,
but habitually? To that question the answer of the Christian
humanist has been and still is that the true and ultimate "vision
of greatness" is the one revealed in Scripture and incarnated in
the person and work of Jesus Christ. Only this, says the Christian humanist, is adequate to serve as the overall perspective.
Nothing else—not the classics or the other humanities, the sciences, or the behavioral sciences—can serve as "the habitual vision of greatness." And if the objection is raised that such a vision is provincial, two things must be said: First, Jesus Christ is
not a denominational figure; of all persons who ever lived he is
incomparably the most important. He is the cosmic Christ. Second, the Bible is the universal book, translated, known, and
read by more people in more lands all over the world than any
other book. For above all, it is the primary written source for
knowledge of Jesus Christ.

"But," someone says, "don't the humanities and the other
fields of learning give perspectives on life; don't they too have

authentic visions, and great ones at that, to offer?" Of course they do. And shortly we shall consider some of the glorious things the humanities can do for us. For the present, however, we are thinking of the essential priority—"the habitual vision of Greatness," spelled, if you will, with a capital "G," while recognizing that the humanities are also "great," though spelled with a small "g," not to belittle them but to signify their very humanness.

The tendency in the Renaissance, a tendency still with us in the secular humanism of our times, was toward placing the humanities and Christianity together as offering jointly and on the same level "the vision of greatness." Again the point is one of priority. All Truth is of God, but not all truth is of the same order or on the same level. It is not the humanities side-by-side with the Scripture that comprise the ultimate and uniting perspective for learning and life. Only the truth revealed in Christ and in Scripture is sufficient for this. Anything less turns us back to the idea that man is "the measure of all things." But for that role man is much too small and inadequate.

When one recognizes this priority, how much there is to see and know and rejoice in! There is an excitement about the humanities that can be very moving. For one thing, the humane visions of greatness in literature and art and music can bring us into encounters with genius. And genius and its products are precious and wonderful things. Genius comes through common grace. As such, it is a miracle of divine sovereignty. In giving genius to a Plato or a Shakespeare; a Leonardo or a Monet; a Mozart or a Tchaikovsky or, to turn again to literature, a Jane Austen or a Hemingway—in doing this, God acted sovereignly and the results of his action are to be accepted thankfully.

How memorable it is to encounter greatness in the humanities! Sometimes it happens through the help of a good teacher, sometimes through a friend, sometimes without any human intermediary. And always the Spirit, who is involved in everything true and beautiful, has his share in it.

To speak at all authentically of these things one must speak personally. So I recall the time in my student days at Harvard when I first read Aristotle's *Poetics*, and felt the invigorating effect of its utter clarity like a cold plunge for my mind. Or there was the afternoon when, as a boy in the fourth grade, I was taken to hear Paderewski in Carnegie Hall and knew for the first time what the piano could sound like—and now, more than sixty years later, his golden tone still rings in my memory. (My mother was responsible for that encounter.) Again I recall how in the forties my friend Emile Cailliet introduced me to the mind of Pascal through the Pensees. And there was the experience in Athens where I worked with a group of scholars on the translation of Isaiah, Job, and Psalms for the New International Version of the Bible and encountered anew the overpowering greatness of the Word of God. How many and how vivid such memories are—encounters over the years with Rembrandt and Cezanne, Chartres Cathedral, with Bach's B-Minor Mass, with Beethoven's Emperor Concerto (through performing it with orchestra), with Augustine and Bunyan, Jane Austen, Browning, Francois Mauriac, and Aleksander Solzhenitsyn. For those of us who know and love the humanities, life is studded with such experiences.

But there is another way of involvement with greatness. This is the encounter with it through nature. It's here that we are confronted with what Marjorie Nicholson in her *Mountain Gloom and Mountain Glory* refers to as "the aesthetics of the infinite."

Yes, visions of greatness are all around us, but we have to take the trouble to see them. To enjoy "the aesthetics of the infinite" demands something of our time and purpose. You have to go to where you are camping and set up your camp there. To get to the top of a mountain you have to put one foot after another till you reach the top. To see the sunrise you have to get up at dawn, and to look at the stars you must step out of your house at night.

So effort has to accompany the use of the humanities. In a lecture in Washington, Antal Dorati, conductor of the National Symphony Orchestra, remarked that an artist must live "a lean life." Likewise it takes leanness in the sense of keeping culturally and spiritually in training to be an intellectual to the glory of God. Formal education is only the beginning. The test of being a genuinely educated person comes not at graduation but at least twenty years later. What do our homes tell of our intellectual and cultural interests? Said Rudyard Kipling in "They," which is one of his most subtle short stories: "Men and women may sometimes, after great effort, achieve a creditable lie; but the house, which is their temple, cannot say anything save the truth of those who have lived in it." The books on our shelves and read in our homes, the records collected and listened to, the pictures chosen and looked at—these have something to say about us.

In the introductory essay to *The Man Born to be King*, Dorothy Sayers used the phrase "the snobbery of the banal." To be candid, it's surprising how many college and university graduates it applies to. Those who cultivate this reverse snobbery look down on great music, old or new, as highbrow; decry serious drama as worldly, yet contentedly watch second-rate television shows; prefer the piously sentimental in their reading; have difficulty distinguishing a kind of religious calendar art from honest art; and sometimes even confuse religious entertainment with worship. It is by the little things that we become what we are, intellectually and culturally as well as in character—and the two should not be divorced. We can't expend most of our leisure on trivia and expect to develop mental muscle any more than we can maintain physical muscle tone without exercise. To be a Christian humanist while at the same time giving in to what Sir Arnold Lunn called "the cult of softness" is impossible. We need to take a critical look at our use of leisure. To be sure we can't always be reading great books, listening to symphonies and grand operas, or wrestling with philosophy. Everyone needs recreation, but it is the quality of our recreation that reveals who we are.

In the writings of John Cassian (300-435 A.A.) there is a charming tradition about the apostle John in his later years at Ephesus. One day while the aged saint was gently stroking a pet partridge, a young man who had just come in from hunting, said, "I'm surprised to see an illustrious man like you doing something so unimportant." To which the apostle replied, "What's that in your hand?" "My bow," said the hunter. "Well," John continued, "if it was always bent, it would lose its elasticity and power. So I need this relief for my mind lest it lose its spring."

There is such a thing as the obligation to discriminate in what we read and see and do, and for this the humanities help develop standards. Too much cultural fat leads to mental flabbiness; too much heavy meat to indigestion; too many sweets lead to insipidity; and if minds and spirits are fed on carrion—and there's plenty of it around these days—this is bound to lead to decay and putridity. The humanities, lofty as their potential can be—and it's not infrequently reached now as in the past, for not everything first rate is old—are capable of decadence, because human beings are fallen creatures. From the tower of Babel and all that preceded it, on through the golden calf and the whole story of idolatry in its protean forms, human history down to our times is full of man's sinning aesthetically and intellectually. To be among those who, as Lewis Mumford has said, "refuse to realize that this is not a normal period . . . it is a terrible time of demoralization and disintegration," is to refuse to face reality.

Literature and the arts, simply because they are so close to our humanness, cannot escape corruption. They can be dehumanized. In speaking of the distortion of the human face and figure in modern art, Jacques Maritain declared, "Modern painting is in possession of every means to express spirituality, save the most normal one"—the face, which he calls "the visible sign and the natural sacrament of human personality . . . because in it an immortal soul shines through." And Wylie Sypher in *The Loss of Self in Modern Literature and Art* probes the same tendency toward disintegration of the human. So the Christian humanist must cultivate a kind of tough-minded critique of literature and art. In his essay on "Religion and Literature," T. S. Eliot said, "What I believe to be incumbent upon all Christians is the duty to maintaining consciously certain standards and criteria of criticism over and above those applied by the rest of the world; and that by these standards and criteria everything that we read must be tested." It's not censorship that's in view here, but the attitude Milton referred to in the *Aeropagitica*, when he spoke of those who can "see and know and yet abstain."

This essay, however, has been considering the humanities at their best when they provide us with excellent models and authentic visions of greatness. Therefore, it is fitting to close on a positive note. The heritage of the humanities is a great and expanding one. It is among the things, to use New Testament words, that God "richly provides us with . . . for our enjoyment," and we avoid or neglect this heritage at the cost of impoverishing the quality of our life.

The scope of the intellectual and cultural life is wonderfully spacious. Paul's words in Philippians may well provide a charter for Christian humanism: "Whatever is true, whatever is noble, whatever is right, whatever is pure, whatever is lovely, whatever is admirable—if anything is excellent or praiseworthy—think about such things." Or as the Jerusalem Bible translates the verb, "fill your minds with" these things. Six categories of things to fill the mind with and nourish it on! And the first one—"the true"—governs all the others. It's a gloriously positive imperative and it includes the inescapable obligation of seeing and judging all things in the perspective of truth. For the Christian humanist today this is a life-long adventure, a continuing story of unflagging interest.

Subject Index

and mountain climbing, 231
prayer life of, 21-22
reading of, 42
Renaissance man, 13
and social issues, 44
wife's influence on, 33-37
Genet, Jean, 94
Gifts
Calvin Seerveld on, 99-100
God and, 61, 176
natural, 65
spiritual, 65, 99
stewardship of, 99
God
as creator, 72
nature of, 58-59
sovereignty of, 75, 76, 176
Grace
common, 66, 75-76, 252
special, 75
Great commission, 62
Grunewald, Matthias, 137

Handel, Georg Friedrich, 136
Harmony, 96
Hayes, Helen, 84-85
Heart, 113
Henry, Carl F. H., 239, 242
Hodge, Charles, 191
Holy Spirit
and the arts, 106
indwelling, 91
inner witness, 226
Humanism
Christian, 14-16, 192, 247-56
secular, 14, 250
Humanities, 127
Humility, 96
Hymns, 135, 168

Image of God, 72, 74, 151, 248, 250
Imagination, 83
Incarnation, 62
Inerrancy, 23, 125
Inevitability, 92
Integrity, 38, 81, 82, 90, 92, 193-94

Intellectual life
biblical teaching, 151, 152-53
call to, 152
Christ-centered, 156
importance of, 151
renewing of, 114
responsibility for, 112
scope of, 153
Sir William Ramsay on, 152
stewardship, 112
Ironside, Harry, 191

Jerome, 172
Jesus Christ
and aesthetics, 64-65
commitment to, 147
and education, 124
and excellence, 144
Lordship, 227
and mountains, 230
paintings, 137, 138
as truth, 153
use of art, 91
as Word of God, 128
Jones, W. Paul, 55-56

Keats, John, 92
Kipling, Rudyard, 55, 254

Leisure, use of, 53, 67, 225-28
Lewis, C. S., 91-92, 191
Liberty, 113
Lincoln, Abraham, 189-90
Literature
Bible and, 189
classic, 197
contemporary, 54
influence of, 57
and King James Bible, 185
T. S. Eliot on, 101-2
Love, 148
Luther, Martin, 131, 132

Machen, J. Gresham, 191
Man (generic term)
and aesthetics, 72-73
Calvin on, 76